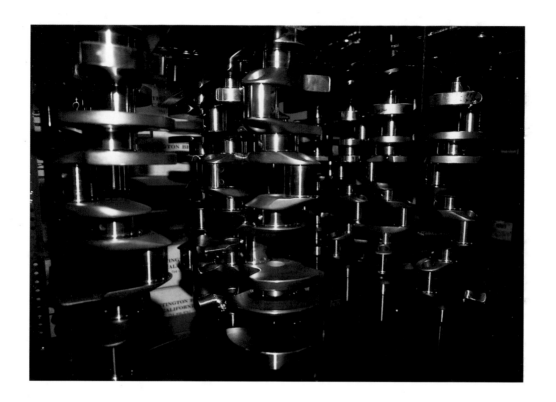

STOCK CAR
RACE FAN'S
REFERENCE GUIDE
UNDERSTANDING NASCAR

William Burt

MBI Publishing Company

Memorial Day is the best racing weekend of the year. As we sit back, party, relax, and enjoy the races, please remember that the cost of this freedom was paid in blood. This book is dedicated to the soldiers that died in faraway places and the soldiers that came home, leaving part of themselves in faraway places, so that the rest of us can enjoy the freedom that they have won.

ACKNOWLEDGMENTS

A special thanks to Mike Rompf, Rich Baron, Paul Wise, Keri Wright, Tina, Mack, Rebecca, Rozelle, and last, but not least, Burns Johns for explaining the principle of words and pictures.

First published in 1999 by MBI Publishing Company,
729 Prospect Avenue, PO Box 1, Osceola, WI 54020-0001 USA

The information in this book is true and complete to the best of our
knowledge. All recommendations are made without any guarantee on the part
of the author or Publisher, who also disclaim any liability incurred in
connection with the use of this data or specific details.

We recognize that some words, model names and designations, for example,
mentioned herein are the property of the trademark holder. We use them for
identification purposes only. This is not an official publication.

MBI Publishing Company books are also available at discounts in bulk
quantity for industrial or sales-promotional use. For details write to Special
Sales Manager at Motorbooks International Wholesalers & Distributors, 729
Prospect Avenue, Osceola, WI 54020-0001 USA.

All photography, unless otherwise noted, is by the author.

Library of Congress Cataloging-in-Publication Data

Burt, William.
Stock car race fan's reference guide: understanding NASCAR/William Burt.
  p. cm.
Includes index.
ISBN 0-7603-0509-9 (alk. paper)
1. Stock car racing--United States. 2. NASCAR (Association) 3. Automobiles,
Racing--United States. I. Title.
GV1029.9.S74B876   1999
796.72'0973--dc21   98-46887

On the front cover: (Top): The Pennzoil Team in action in 1997. During a pit stop, only seven men are allowed over the wall. Look closely, seven Pennzoil members are working to save seconds during this tire change and fuel topping.

(Left): Different tracks offer different conveniences. Bristol, for example, offers the convenience of natural-light work areas—there are no garages for the teams! As seen in this photo, the teams line their cars up side-by-side, put them on jack stands, open the hoods, and begin their work (rain or shine).

(Right): Some areas of the car are more vulnerable than others. Damage to the left front where the oil cooler is mounted can be fatal, whereas the same damage to the right front (as with the Tide Taurus at Bristol) would still permit the car to continue racing.

On the frontispiece: Want to go racing? The budget for crankshafts alone is more than many fans make in a year!

On the title page: Sunday morning finds many teams still at work. The cars, or at least the windshields, are covered to keep the interior cool. A cart with a generator accompanies each car to provide power for heaters that keep the oil warm. Once the cars are on the starting grid, they won't be cranked up until the race begins.

On the back cover: (Top): As some crew members are setting up the pit, others are still preparing the car. Everything on the car is checked before the car goes to inspection. Once a car clears inspection, it will go to the starting grid.

(Bottom): Early Sunday morning on race day, the teams begin to set up their pit stall. Each team has its own style of pit cart that contains just about everything the team anticipates needing during the race, including tools, spare parts, and in some cases, even a television.

Edited by John Adams-Graf
Designed by Bruce Leckie

Printed in Hong Kong through World Print, Ltd.

CONTENTS

Chapter 1   THE CARS   9

Chapter 2   THE TEAMS   81

Chapter 3   THE SHOPS   97

Chapter 4   THE SETUP   113

Chapter 5   AT THE TRACK   127

Chapter 6   RULES AND REFERENCE   159

Index   191

INTRODUCTION

Most of us grew up playing sports. Whether it was football, baseball, volleyball, or bowling, many of us actively participated in some type of sport. And we learned. If, for example, you played football when you were growing up, you know that on third down with a foot to go, the percentage play is to run up the middle. In baseball, with a runner on first and no outs, a good call is to have the batter bunt in order to advance the runner into scoring position. Over time, we learned to recognize the appropriateness of these plays when the coach called them.

In racing, however, it is different. Very few of us grew up racing automobiles (I wish it had been offered as a high school sport!). As a result, very few of us know what really goes into having a successful racing program other than having a good driver. Few really know all about the cars' construction and what the teams do before and during a race to make their cars more competitive. We don't really know what options are out there to make the cars go faster. Many of us are somewhat familiar with the street versions of the Winston Cup cars, but very unfamiliar with the actual Cup cars. We see the teams at the track or on television (mainly during pit stops), but don't know what they do the rest of the time. Many don't know that on race day, the crew we see at the race is just part of the team. Many team members who work on the cars don't even come to the track. They are at home watching the race on television like we are. Fans get very few looks at the business side of racing—all of the things that must happen just to assemble the team and get the car to the track. These are the reasons for this book.

If you are new to the sport and want a more complete understanding of Winston Cup racing, this is a good place to start. This book is a guide to help the average fan understand the more technical side of Winston Cup racing. A more complete understanding of any sport makes it more enjoyable to watch.

I fell asleep during the first race that I attended (Talladega 1970), my only excuse being that I was seven. But I loved it and became a fan. And over the past few years, millions of others have also become fans.

There has been much discussion as to why the Winston Cup Series has become so popular. Over lunch a few years ago, Bobby Allison explained that the reason he thought NASCAR had become so popular was not the speed, color, or excitement (though all were contributing factors); rather, he said, the single most important reason for the sport's popularity was the common bond of driving. Everybody either drives a car, has driven a car, or is waiting to be old

Three-wide racing at 200 miles per hour has become commonplace in Winston Cup racing. If it is possible to fit three cars into a turn, the drivers will do it. You don't see that in Formula One.

enough to drive a car. I am a golfer and if I try hard enough (and I mean really hard) I can imagine myself playing with the guys on tour. I played football and can visualize myself playing at Auburn for the SEC championship (too many strikes and labor problems among the millionaires who play the game professionally!). Anyhow, having played these sports, it is easy for me to make the connection with the game. I think that is Bobby Allison's idea of the common bond that a race fan has with Winston Cup racing. Anyone who drives a street car, pickup truck, or mini van can visualize themselves diving under the leader as they come out of turn four to take the win. I know that I can.

Winston Cup racing is a sport in which circumstance can play as much a role as preparation as talent. Very few pro golfers who have been leading a tournament have been forced to withdraw because someone in thirtieth position broke his putter. Likewise, no football teams have been unable to continue in the fourth quarter because of shoulder-pad failure. Intangible factors are what allow a car to win. The same intangibles can also take the fastest car on the track out of the race at any time. Any way you look at it, the action never stops until the checkered flag waves.

CHAPTER 1

Weighing nearly twice as much as many types of race cars, Winston Cup cars must be caressed around the track. If the cars are over-driven, the tires will overheat and handling will suffer.

THE CARS

CAR INTRODUCTION

Race cars are out there that are much faster than Winston Cup cars. With a steel chassis, steel body, pushrod V-8 power, and a solid rear axle, Winston Cup cars are on the cutting edge of "yesterday's technology." Cup cars do not rely on breakthrough technologies in order to increase speed and handling. There are no carbon-fiber chassis, 12,000-rpm motors, or aerodynamic wings that keep the car sucked to the track. That's not to say that fielding a successful Winston Cup team is not as difficult as fielding an Indy, Cart, or Formula One team—it is. It's just a different way of going at it. In order to get more speed, Winston Cup crews must continually refine existing technology against changing track conditions. The tools for that job are experience, imagination, and hard work.

Winston Cup cars are some of the most durable in the world of automobile racing. Impacts that would take many race cars out of a race may have no effect in the performance of Cup cars.

Winston Cup cars must be built within certain specifications established by NASCAR. These specifications eliminate many of today's exotic materials and designs for everything but the safety systems of the car. Concepts and systems seen in other racing venues, such as turbochargers, overhead cam configurations, advanced aerodynamics, in-car computer telemetry, and extensive use of special materials such as carbon fiber, are not allowed in Winston Cup racing. This forces teams to rely on better engineering of old technology and to give more attention to the car's race setup.

Winston Cup teams make many small changes to the cars and engines that, when looked at alone, may not seem to help very much. But when all of these small changes are added together, they may be the difference between winning and being an also-ran.

Today's rules not only provide for safe and very competitive racing on the track, they also set the stage for another competition—the constant race within the shops, practice sessions, and wind tunnels where the teams learn more and more about the forces that their race cars encounter and the components on the cars that counter those forces. By constantly "tweaking" and fine-tuning each component and system on the race car, the teams achieve more and more speed every year. Many times in the past, the rules have been changed to slow the cars down, forcing the engineers to continue to search for changes which still give that small but important advantage on the track. It seems, though, every time a rule is made to slow the cars down, the teams massage the cars and recover the speed that the rules changes took away. A recent example of this is a rule that lowered engine compression. Beginning in 1998, all engines were required to have a maximum of 12:1 compression, down from the 14:1 compression ratios run in 1997. While this slowed speeds for a few races, by midseason the cars were as fast as they had ever been.

Three makes of cars currently compete on the Winston Cup Circuit: the Chevrolet Monte Carlo, the Ford Taurus, and the Pontiac Grand

Ready for the officials to open the track for practice.

The search for the perfect setup never ends. Until the cars have to be on the starting grid, the teams work on their cars, checking and rechecking everything.

Prix. These are not the only models allowed, however. Buick, Mercury, and Oldsmobile also have approved models, but due to a variety of factors, none now run on the circuit. While Winston Cup cars do look somewhat like the production cars after which they are named, they have very little in common other than the name. Only a few parts are actually identical to the production models.

BUILDING A WINSTON CUP CAR

Other than the engine and sheet-metal body, all cars are pretty much the same. The days of starting with a production car and converting it to a race car are long gone. Modern Winston Cup cars are hand-built from metal tubing, fabrications, sheet metal, and after-market racing products. The relationship of a Winston Cup car to the manufacturer is generally only skin deep. There is more than one car out there

that has changed from Ford to Chevy or from Chevy to Ford and back again.

Winston Cup cars are required to weigh a minimum of 3,400 lb ready to race, with all fluids and without the driver. On a circle track, the more weight on the inside of the car, the better it will handle. To regulate this, NASCAR has

The Pontiac Grand Prix.

The Chevrolet Monte Carlo.

dictated that the right side of the car must weigh at least 1,600 lb. On road courses, crews must set the car up with a minimum weight of 1,600 lb on both the left and right sides. Weight is also added to the car to equalize driver weight. For drivers weighing less than 200 lb, weight is added in 10 lb increments until the total hits at least 200 lb. If a driver weighs 195 lb, 10 lb will be added. A driver weighing 155 lb

gets another 50 lb.

Cars are built as light a possible. When it is necessary to add weight to the car, it is in the form of blocks weighing at least 5 lb and bolted inside the body in an approved (by NASCAR officials) position. Car weight is monitored closely. When the car is weighed after the race, oil, water, and gas may be added but the wheels cannot be changed. One-half of one percent of the car's weight is added for the after-race weigh-in to compensate for wear experienced during the race.

Cars are weighed after the race to make sure that teams have not purposely "lost" weight during the race. A team once used lead shot to make the car weigh-in before the race and released it during the race to lighten up the car.

The Ford Taurus.

A car begins to take shape. Winston Cup cars are nothing less than hand-built masterpieces.

BUILDING THE CHASSIS/ROLL CAGE

The tremendous strength of the frame and roll cage assembly is the cornerstone of driver safety. High-strength steel coupled with a philosophy of "overbuild it—don't underbuild it" is the reason for the incredible strength. In the past, teams bought their frame and cage assemblies from suppliers. Nowadays, however, most premier teams build their assemblies inhouse. This enables the teams to experiment with the chassis geometry. Suspension mounting points can be altered and the chassis can be built with one type of track in mind. NASCAR monitors the chassis, though. All frames must have an identification code stamped on the right side of the main roll bar. The code indicates the builder, the date of manufacture, and the sequence number.

The frame rails are the innermost, bottom frame components. Made from square carbon steel tubing with a minimum length of 65 in., the frame rails must be built parallel to each other. Offset chassis are not permitted. Side rails must be inserted in standard rocker panels and must be of steel box tubing 3 in. wide by 4 in. high, with a wall thickness of .120 in. The minimum distance between the frame side rails, measured inside to inside, can be no less than 50 in.

Lead blocks waiting to be put into the car. Race cars are built lighter than the minimum weight rule so the teams may put weight where they want it, which will affect the car's handling.

The regulations further stipulate that the front and rear subframes must be steel material 2 in. wide and 3 in. high. Cross members (the pieces that tie the frame together) and other pieces are made of 2 in.-by-2 in. tubing (also .120 in. thick). All connections attaching the frame together are welded.

NASCAR dictates dimensions, placement, and the type of assembly of the roll cage with directions and diagrams and instructions provided in the rule book. The rules require round, seamless, steel-tubing 1 3/4 in.-by-.090 in. roll bars. All roll bar connections must be welded, and all bars within the driver's reach must be padded.

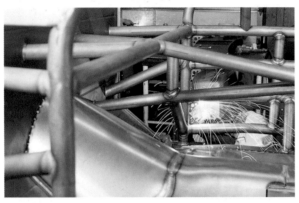

Many feet of weld will be required to complete the chassis/roll cage.

The finished product of the welder.

Sections of the roll cage/chassis are built on jigs. The jig is the starting point of the chassis. Using it as a fixture to construct the chassis, builders can build one nearly identical chassis after another. Or one with only the variations that they want. The variations that teams don't know about are the ones that cause handling problems.

The entire unit is then assembled on the surface plate. It is critical for the builders to know that the foundation on which they build their cars is solid and true.

Suspension fittings are added to the frame rails. For the finished car to handle properly, all of these must be positioned correctly. A mistake at this point could mean a handling problem that will have to be overcome on the track.

Small flanges are added to provide extra strength around connections. All welded connections must be "clean," with no sharp edges.

Once the foundation of the chassis is complete, it can be put on a rolling carriage so that the entire car can be completed. This allows another car to be put on the surface plate and also allows the chassis to be moved easily through the shop.

The strength of the Cup cars comes from the assembly of the roll cage. Side bars protect the driver from side impacts, potentially one of the most dangerous types of accidents.

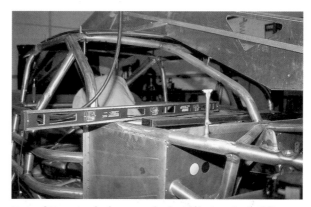

Everything must be kept on the level during the building process.

The rear of the chassis. Note the wheelwells and the steel tub for the fuel cell.

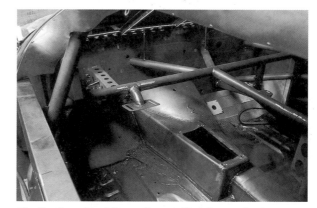

The floorboard and firewall are added during the chassis-building process.

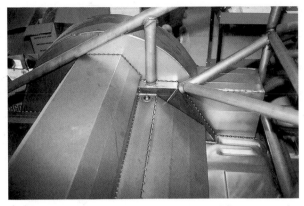

Roll bars must pass through the sheetmetal floor pan and the firewall to the frame rails. All other sheetmetal pieces are added after the chassis is completed.

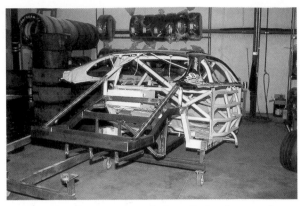

Winston Cup chassis are tough. Even if a car is severely damaged, the chassis can be repaired. Here, a new rear clip has just been added, and in a few weeks this car will be ready to go back on the track.

ASSEMBLING THE BODY

Body assembly begins at the top. The roof template is set, the roof is mounted, and the car is assembled in a downward direction. A standard suspension is mounted to the chassis during the body-building process.

When the roof is done, the hood and deck lid (shown here) are welded and riveted into place.

The front fascia is mounted. A tubular frame supports it and holds it in place.

The fenders, door area, and quarter panels come next. These pieces are handmade from sheet metal.

Most body panels begin as a piece of sheet metal. Only parts of the hood, roof, and deck lid are factory parts.

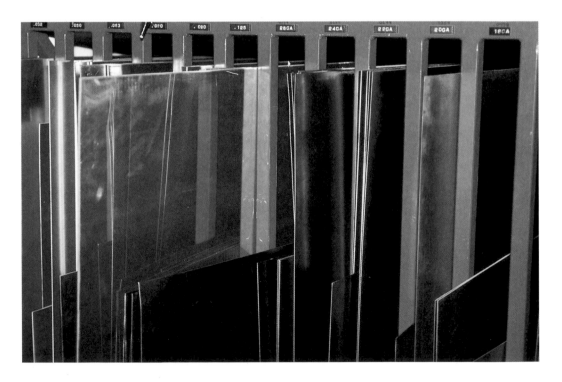

The shape of the piece being made (here a fender) is drawn on the sheet metal.

More precise cuts are hand clipped.

Then the pieces are rolled and fitted to shape.

Body panels are mounted with rivets and welded together. Once finished, they will become a slick, aerodynamic one-piece unit.

Winston Cup cars are nothing short of handmade steel works of art. Throughout the fabrication process the body panel is checked against the car.

The rear fascia completes the "lower body."

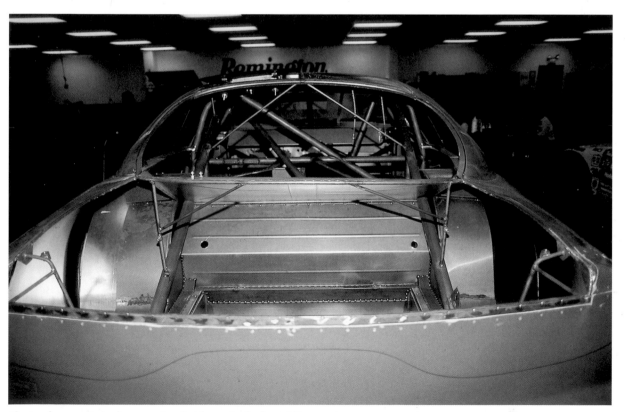

The trunk area. Note the supports that keep the body stable.

Roof pillars during construction. After assembly there is a great deal of finishing work to be done to get the car ready to paint. It may look kind of rough now, but by the time the car gets to the track not a seam will be visible.

Measure twice and cut once. During the assembly process, countless measurements are taken to ensure the car is being built as planned.

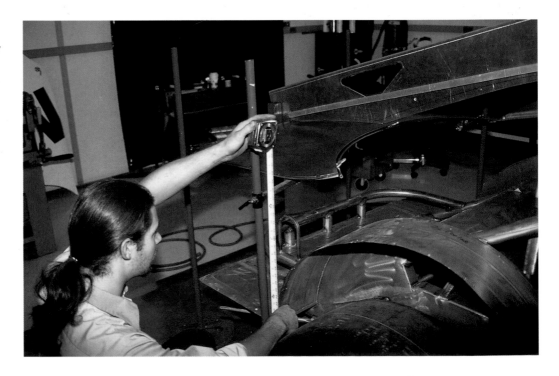

Throughout the building process, templates are used to make sure the body fits NASCAR rules. Each team has a full set of templates for each part of the body.

Grinding off the welds begins the smoothing process.

The bodywork begins. All of the seams and attachment points will have slick surfaces. After the body is finished, it is primered, and then suspension, cockpit, engine, and drivetrain will be added. The car is cleaned for painting. It has been sanded slick and cleaned.

Only the best paints touch a Winston Cup car.

After painting, the last mechanical touches are put on the car.

Stickers come last. This car will have the motor put in and be ready to go to the track. (Unfortunately, the track in this case was Pocono, where the crew cut down a tire and the car got into the wall. That's racing. Build a masterpiece and bad luck tears it up. While this may be depressing, it does provide job security for the car builders.)

BODY COMPONENTS

Although it is much lighter and aerodynamically more efficient than the multi-piece factory front ends, the front fascia must be strong enough to handle some pretty severe abuse and keep on functioning.

Front Fascia

Made of Kevlar, the front fasciae (or nose pieces) on Winston Cup cars are not the same as found on production cars. The dimensions of the front fasciae are established before the season begins to ensure that no model gains an

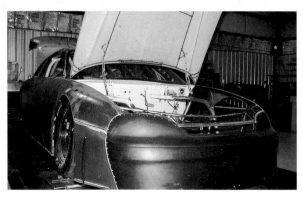

The front fascia before bodywork and painting.

unfair advantage by converting the multiple-piece production-car fascia to a one-piece racing fascia. The front fascia is mounted on a frame of square tubing fabricated during the building of the chassis. Each front fascia has an individual serial number. No team is permitted to alter the shape or contours to improve aerodynamic flow. Openings are cut into the front of the fascia to allow air to be ducted to various systems that require cooling. The grill openings used are covered by two layers of wire screen. These screens, used for protection from debris, are attached to the grill. No devices that direct airflow may be placed between the grill and the radiator.

The grill area is of critical importance and must do a number of things at one time. As the leading edge of the car, the fascia is critical for good aerodynamic flow. Grills must allow enough air in to cool the engine. At the same time, however, the team has to be mindful that

The front fascias are monitored closely by NASCAR officials. Each fascia must retain the factory serial number.

too large an opening will create drag and lift the front end of the car at high speeds. Grill openings are also used to duct air to the brake rotors. This is a distinct advantage on tracks that are demanding on brakes. Air is also ducted from the left grill opening to the oil cooler, which is mounted inside the left front fender in front of the left front tire. Overheating of the brakes or the oil is likely if these openings are closed due to damage or debris.

Hood

All teams must use factory-produced hood skins. Original support panels holding the sheet-metal hood rigid are replaced with custom supports made from 1/2 in. square steel tubing. The hinges fold back to keep the hood open. When closed, the hood is locked into position with four positive pin fasteners (hood pins). The fasteners are evenly spaced along the front of the hood. The air intake for the carburetor is located on the centerline of the car, between the back of the hood and front of the windshield.

A clean hood profile is necessary for good airflow over the car on longer tracks. If the

At super speedways more of the grill intake area is taped off. This eliminates drag and improves the downforce on the front of the car. Also, it is not necessary to cool the brakes on super speedways.

hood is damaged, the disturbed airflow will affect the car's aerodynamics and slow it. Short-track performance is usually not affected much by cosmetic hood damage, but it is true that the only time aerodynamics don't matter is when the car is sitting still.

Roof

Stock roof panels designated for the make and model of the car being raced are mandatory. The height, shape, and size of the roof cannot change. Airflow over the roof is of critical importance. It influences the way the air

On short-track cars the grill is not taped. At the lower speeds, the lifting effect of the open ducts is not as great. Also, with all the rubber that is built up on short tracks, it's a good idea to have as much area open as possible to cool the engine and brakes.

hits the rear spoiler, which in turn affects the way the car handles. Teams go to great lengths to make sure the airflow to the rear spoiler is optimized while still ensuring that the roof profile remains legal. Additionally, two 1/2 in. pieces of aluminum angle must be mounted between the windshield and the rear glass, as far to the outside of the roof as possible. These are used to help stabilize the car at high speeds.

Roof flaps that deploy if the car gets sideways or backward in a spin have become mandatory on all tracks in Winston Cup racing.

The back of a front fascia with ducting still attached. The shroud in the center ducts air to the radiator while the outer ducts funnel air to the brakes.

Possibly the most famous hood in racing. Factory hood skins are required by the NASCAR rules.

Much like it does on an airplane wing, air moving fast across the top of the car creates a low-pressure area. When the car gets turned sideways, this low pressure sucks the roof flaps up. Once activated, the flaps "catch" the air under them and push the car down on the track. This minimizes the amount of air getting under the car and helps to prevent serious crashes, as air under a high-speed race car usually causes it to flip.

Firewall

Firewalls do just what their name implies. They act to protect the driver from the heat of the engine and provide protection during dangerous engine failures. Firewalls are made of 22-gauge steel and must be welded into place. A tunnel is cut through the firewall for the transmission. The tunnel may be no wider than 18 in. at the bottom, and must be at least 10 in. below the leading edge of the windshield. It

The underside of the hood is reinforced with fabricated support frames to keep the hood stable at high speeds. The rules require a system to hold the hood up when it's open.

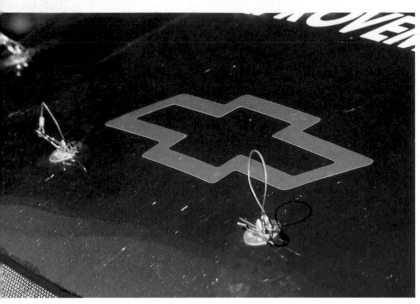

Four hood pins keep the hood secure at high speeds.

No stickers are allowed on the roof—only the car's number.

may not be wider than 10 in. when it passes the driver's seat.

"Crush panels" extend from the firewall to the fenders. The crush panel is another body part that a driver hates to see get damaged during a race. When these panels are damaged, fumes from the engine or other cars can inundate the car's interior, making a 500-mile race seem five times longer.

Doors

Doors don't really exist on modern Winston Cup cars, though the sides maintain the factory contours and accent lines. Drivers get in and out of the car through the driver side window. Instead of a door, Winston Cup cars have a slick, aerodynamic one-piece side, which is hand-crafted in one piece from .025 in. sheet steel. These side pieces cover an area from

The hood profile is always checked by NASCAR officials before qualifying and racing.

Roof flaps were developed to keep the cars from flipping during spins. Before roof flaps were invented, air would get under the car, causing some horrific flips.

about the center of the front wheel to the center of the rear wheel and are riveted and welded in place, with all of the weld seams smoothed.

As it is with all other body pieces on the car, great care is taken to produce the pieces to exacting tolerances. This is more easily said than done, considering the compound curves in the body of a Winston Cup car. When measuring lap speeds down to one-hundredth or one-thousandth of a second, the slightest flaw can upset the aerodynamics of the car and slow it down or affect the handling. The best way to make these parts correctly is to have proper tools and years of experience.

Fenders and Quarter Panels

Filling the area between the sides and the front and rear fasciae are the short, handmade front fender and rear quarter panel. They must be installed in their standard locations as referenced by a production car model. Fenders and quarter panels are altered somewhat to allow for tire clearance. The fuel intake is located on the left quarter panel. A spring-activated valve opens only when the fill tank nozzle is inserted. If the car is competing for "manufacturers' awards," sponsors' stickers are located in precise positions.

Deck Lids

The deck lid (or trunk lid) is one of the few "stock" parts used in a Winston Cup car, and it retains the stock shape, contour, and appearance. When closed, it is held shut with two pin fasteners. Deck lids must have work-

Roof flaps are checked often to make sure they are functional.

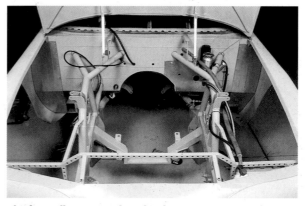

The firewall is mounted as the chassis is constructed. It ensures that engine fumes—and any engine fire—stay in the engine compartment and do not get to the driver.

ing hinges and a self-holding device to keep the lid up when it is open. The stock deck lid backing structure is replaced with custom-fabricated supports that keep the deck lid rigid at high speeds.

Rear Fascia

Manufactured much the same as the front fascia, the rear fascia is built according to standards established by the original equipment manufacturer and NASCAR officials. While keeping the profile and shape roughly the same as that of a production car, the rear body pieces are of one-piece construction and do not include a functional bumper.

Front Air Dam

The air dam's purpose is to keep as much air from going under the car as possible. The more air that goes under the car, the more lift the car will have. As the car goes faster, the lift increases. On long, fast courses, a damaged air dam will result in a slower car that is more difficult to drive. The front air dam ground clearance is established by NASCAR and is one of the changing variables that officials use to even the playing field between different makes of cars. All support brackets holding the air dam in place must be mounted on its back. The leading edge of the air dam may not extend more than 1/2 in. forward of the bumper.

Rear Spoiler

The air passing over the car and onto the rear spoiler is deflected upward, forcing the

Winston Cup cars have no doors. The entire side of the car is made as one solid piece of sheet metal. Drivers and crew access the interior through the driver-side window. The entire side of the car is finished as a slick, aerodynamic one-piece side unit with no visible seams.

Drivers enter and exit through the driver-side window.

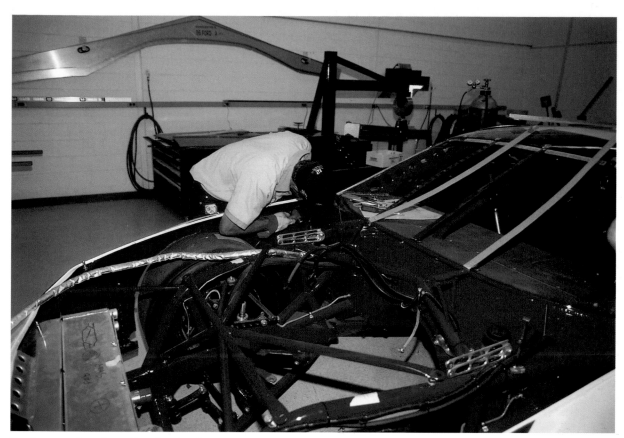

Fenders are altered to allow for tire clearance.

rear of the car down and improving the car's handling ability in the turns. This force is commonly referred to as "downforce."

Made from .125 in.-thick aluminum, rear spoilers are nonadjustable and must be attached to the rear deck lid. The rear spoiler is made in two pieces and mounted with a thin gap on the centerline of the body. This gap is necessary to allow inspection templates to be fitted directly on the car's body when checking

If the car is competing for "manufacturers' awards," the stickers must be located in precise positions. The rule book requires car numbers to be 18 inches high.

The fuel intake is located on the left quarter panel. A spring-activated valve opens only when the fill tank nozzle is inserted.

the profile. All rear spoilers are made of aluminum and mounted so they will not bend or flex under the air pressure encountered when racing. Rear spoilers must be mounted with at least six 1/4 in. or larger bolts across the back of the deck lid. Edges must be cut square and the corners may be rounded to no more than a 1/2 in. radius.

At Talladega and Daytona, officials determine the rear spoiler angle setting that will be used before the race. The rear spoiler angle ensures that the spoiler is mounted high enough to give the cars plenty of downforce, which, in turn, makes for safer racing.

Fender rods keep the fender rigid and allow for some adjustment in the fender profile.

Windshields

All cars must use windshields made of hard-coated polycarbonate material. Three inside metal braces must be bolted (using 1/4 in. bolts) to the roof or roll bar at the top and to the dash panel at the bottom to support the windshield from the inside of the car. Two metal reinforcements must be used on the outside directly in front of the outward, inside supports. The outside reinforcements are stainless-steel 1 in.-wide strips with a rubber gasket between themselves and the windshield. Tinting windows any darker than stock, other than a 6 in. strip along the top, is not allowed. This is enforced because a driver must be able to see through the rear window and windshield of the car he or she is trailing.

The quarter panel becomes the bulletin board while preparing for the race. The "to do" lists are taped up and individual items are checked off when complete.

A rear deck lid being fabricated. Support is added to prevent distortion at high speeds.

The spoiler is attached to the deck lid.

The rear fascia is a one-piece unit designed specially for racing applications.

Side Windows

For tracks less than 1.5 miles and for road courses, side windows (or door windows) must be removed from the cars. In place of the side window, a nylon web screen with a minimum size of 22 in. wide by 16 in. tall is installed in the driver-side door's window opening. These screens are made of 3/4 in.-wide strips. The window screen mounts must be welded to the roll cage.

On tracks more than 1.5 miles, the same screen system is used on the driver's window.

The front air dam is mounted along the bottom edge of the front fascia. Spoiler height is strictly monitored and currently cannot be lower than 5 in.

The rear spoiler provides downforce, which keeps the rear of the car glued to the track. A great deal of attention is paid to it to make sure it meets the rules and performs its best.

The difference, however, is that the cars must have a full window on the right side. This window must be made of 1/4 in. polycarbonate glass. No tape is allowed on the side window glass.

Quarter Windows

Quarter windows (the small window directly behind the door window) remain located in their stock position. Only 1/4 in. polycarbonate glass is used for these windows.

The rear spoiler is supported on the back, preventing it from being "pushed down" by the air at high speeds.

A slot is left in the center of the spoiler so the template can be fitted to the car during inspection.

These windows are not solid: Openings are cut into them to add a bit of extra cooling by "picking up" air to cool the rear brakes and the oil reserve tank.

Rear Window

Made of polycarbonate glass, the rear window on a Winston Cup car is the same thickness and shape as the original glass used for the rear window. A light tint in the window is allowed, but the tint must be light enough to allow trailing drivers to see through the rear window and the windshield. This ensures that drivers' hand signals will be seen when waving or pointing to action taking place on the track.

Two 1/8 in.-thick (minimum) by 1-in.-wide metal straps secure the rear window. These strips are bolted to the roof at the top and to the deck lid support panel at the bottom. Holes are drilled in both sides of the rear window to allow wrenches to be inserted through to the bolts that adjust the "wedge" or rear spring settings.

Windshields are hard polycarbonate material, a much stronger material than factory glass.

Metal straps on the outside of the car help keep the wind-shield on the car, making sure that it does not come out during a spin or collision.

A roll bar runs behind the windshield, along the centerline of the car, to prevent large pieces of debris (like tires) coming through the wind-shield during wrecks.

A super speedway side glass. Side glass is required on all tracks longer than 1 1/2 miles.

Cockpit

Safety and driver comfort are the main priorities when setting up the interior of the race car. All gauges and controls must be positioned so the driver can use them with the least distraction to his driving. Gauges are usually mounted so that when all of the needles are pointing straight up everything is Okay. Two ignition systems are mounted to the right of the driver. The backup ignition activator switch must be within easy reach.

As indicated before, all roll bars within the driver's reach are padded. This protects the driver during crashes. A complete fire extinguishing system is also installed for the driver's personal safety. The driver's seating position is a custom fit. Each driver has preferences for seat angle and height. Some drivers like to sit more upright, close to the steering wheel. Others sit low in the car in a more reclined position. Steering wheel size is also a matter of driver preference.

No passenger-side glass is required on short tracks. Note the "air pickup" vent in the lower front corner. Quarter windows are used to "pick up" air for brake and oil cooling on some tracks.

The driver-side window is covered with a window net. Enough room is left open in the lower front corner to pass the driver fluids during the race.

On super speedways a "flush" window will be run for aerodynamic reasons.

Above is a Ford Taurus rear window; below is a Chevrolet Monte Carlo rear window. Drivers must be able to see hand signals from the drivers in front of them.

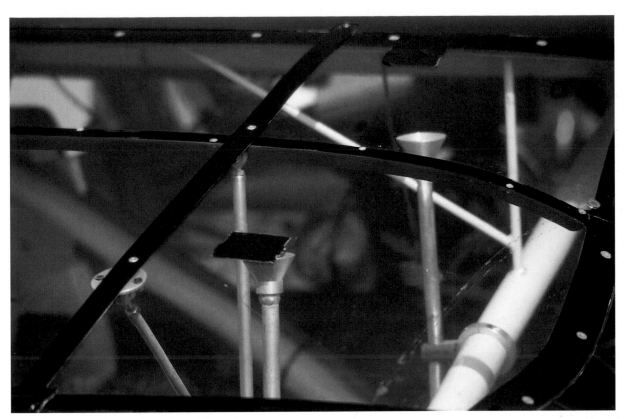

Note the openings for wedge and track bar adjustments.

The driver's office. Gauges must be laid out so engine systems can be monitored at a glance. Gauge layout varies from car to car.

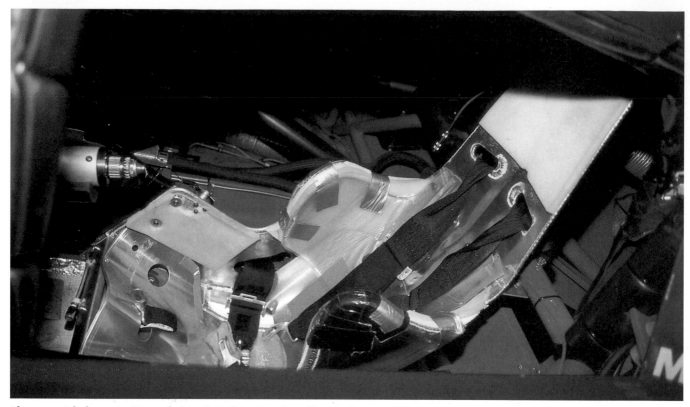

The seat with the cover removed. Seats are custom made to fit each driver.

Both ignition units are located in the cockpit with the driver to help protect them.

All roll bars within the driver's reach must be padded.

THE ENGINE

In Winston Cup racing, only small-block V-8 engines are allowed. For Chevy, that means a 350, and for Ford, a 351. Regardless of which is used, the engine must be built to have a displacement between 350 and 358 cubic inches and a maximum compression ratio of 12.0:1 (pronounced "twelve to one").

The motor cannot be located farther back than the centerline of the forward-most spark plug hole on the right side cylinder head, in line with the upper ball-joint. Additionally, the centerline of the crankshaft must be on the centerline of the tread width (equidistant from both front wheels). From the center of the crankshaft to the ground, a minimum of 10 in. is mandatory. All motor mounts must be made of steel and cannot be adjustable.

Blocks

Most blocks used in Winston Cup Racing are manufactured by the race divisions of General Motors or Ford. Specifically made for racing, these blocks do not appear in any production vehicle. The material is cast iron—aluminum blocks are not allowed.

Engines start with a longer stroke and smaller cylinder diameter (bore x bore x .7854 x stroke = displacement of one cylinder). As a block is worn and is bored out, the stroke is shortened as the bore increases to achieve the desired displacement. By employing this method, blocks can be used for a relatively long period of time. Some two- and three-year-old blocks are still racing. Racing blocks differ from the production blocks in that they have thicker cylinder walls to eliminate distortion and give a better surface for the rings. Improved water passages increase the cooling ability. Adding bulkhead material to the main bearing bosses adds strength around the crankshaft. Increased strength around the

Epoxy filling in the blocks is allowed. This is done to help the oil flow efficiently in the block.

Four-bolt main caps are used to hold the crankshaft in place in Cup motors. Note the way the bolts are "splayed" outward to increase the strength of the cap.

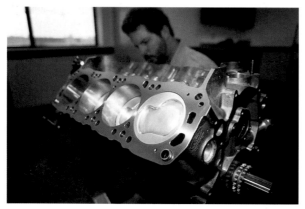

A "bottom end" ready to go. The crankshaft, pistons, rods, and bearings have all been installed.

A Winston Cup crankshaft. The force applied to this piece of equipment is incredible. If anything goes wrong here, the team's day is over.

The front of the crankshaft after installation. The gear will drive the timing chain.

Rods are tough pieces of equipment that can be used in more than one race. Heavy H-beam-style rods are used.

A set of pistons ready to be installed.

The combustion chamber of a cylinder head. The large intake and exhaust valve seats are visible.

The top of the piston has been machined to allow for valve clearance.

The top of the bare cylinder head. This is where the valve train will be installed.

deck surface where the heads bolt on increases engine stability. Blocks have four-bolt main-bearing caps.

Because of NASCAR rules the following may *not* be changed:

- Material
- Number of cylinders
- Angle of cylinders
- Number and type of main bearings
- Integral or separate cylinder sleeves
- Location of camshaft
- Overall configuration

Note: The same block that started the race must finish it.

Crankshafts

Most crankshafts are 4340 alloy steel forgings, made by after-market sources, although there are still a few billet-machined crankshafts in use. Only steel crankshafts are allowed but they may be lightened and balanced. Approved harmonic balancers (bolt-on balancing devices)

are also allowed. The crankshaft lobes are tapered on the leading edges to reduce windage (drag created by the front edge of the crankshaft lobes passing through the air and oil in the block) allowing the engine to spin easier, thereby increasing horsepower.

Teams use various brands of high-quality bearings. Because the tolerances between the crank and the bearing are very precise, engine builders may take as long as a day to install main bearings, making sure of a tight, clean fit. If the fit is too loose, there will be too much movement and the engine may fail. If it is too tight, there will not be enough space for the oil to properly lubricate the crank, and again engine failure may result.

Connecting Rods

The rules allow only steel connecting rods. Most are forged, H-beam-style rods that are heavy and very strong. Engine builders tend not to compromise on the quality of the rods, not wanting to risk strength for a small perform-

The camshaft being installed in the engine.

The cylinder head mounted on the engine.

ance gain by using a lighter rod. Heavy rod bolts are used to attach the rod caps. Many Chevys and Fords use identical rods. No stainless-steel or titanium rods are allowed.

Pistons

Winston Cup cars may use any type of aluminum piston. Most are forged and designs vary from team to team. Pistons take an incredible pounding during 500 miles of racing. With the high compression and intense combustion pressures experienced in a racing engine, pistons will occasionally fail. Fans will often hear of a driver "burning a piston." This is a piston failure in which a hole is literally burned through the top of the piston. Pistons used in Winston Cup racing cars are not "flat topped," though. The piston crowns have domes, which help to increase compression. They must be "fly-cut" or "relieved" to provide clearance for the valves that share space in the combustion chamber with the piston domes. When the valves are off their seats, they cannot contact the rising piston or the engine will self-destruct.

Cylinder Heads

All Winston Cup heads are aluminum. Recent changes in the rules have limited the available heads to one Ford and one General Motors head design, either Ford part number E3ZM6049C3, dated 9/9/91 or later, or for GM cars, Chevrolet part number 10134364, casting number 10134363.

Valve location and angle must remain stock. By changing the angle and location, teams can change the geometry of the head and thus the combustion chamber. This can build horsepower and gives some teams an advantage over others, but is very expensive. Spacing between valves (center to center) is 1.935 in. for Chevrolet and 1.900 in. for Ford. Internal polishing and porting (that is, custom machining the intake and exhaust ports on the cylinder head to match the manifold ports) are allowed. Rules strictly limit the modifications, which, in turn, ensures that the heads will be less expensive and more durable, and that racing will remain competitive.

The following may not be changed on cylinder heads:
· Material
· Number of valves per cylinder
· Type of combustion chamber
· Location of spark plug

Only solid lifters are allowed by NASCAR. Lifters ride on the camshaft, "lifting" on the lobes of the cam, which provides the energy to open and close the valves.

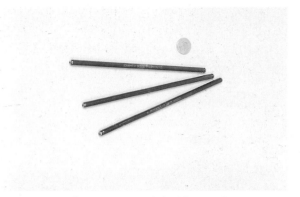

Push rods transfer the motion of the lifter to the rocker arms.

· Orientation of spark plug
· Arrangement of valves
· Type of valve actuation
· Number of intake ports
· Number of exhaust ports
· Center distances of intake ports
· Center distances of exhaust ports
· Shape of ports at mating surface of manifolds
· Angle of port face relative to mating surface of head to block
· Firing order

Camshafts

Teams look for a camshaft that is durable while providing an acceptable amount of power. The lobe designs of General Motors and Ford camshafts are similar, but there are differences between the two. The Ford camshaft is shorter and thicker. This design is inherently stronger than the GM camshafts, which are longer and narrower. Because of this design difference, many times the Ford and GM camshafts are made using different materials.

Camshaft durability is so important that teams may run the same camshaft at many different non-restricter plate tracks, relying on intake ports, headers, and intake manifolds to change the "powerband" of the engine to fit the particular track. A camshaft has to be many things at once. A cam has to be hard in the lobe area for resistance to friction, but must be "soft" enough to flex a little and not snap and break. It is very difficult to produce a camshaft that fits these requirements.

When camshafts break, they tend to break at the rear, which is the longest section without support. Because of this, Chevrolet cams are usually made from 8620 alloy steel, with stel-

Rocker arms change the upward motion of the push rod to the downward motion required to open and close the valves.

lite (an extremely wear-resistant alloy) welded to the lobes. The 8620 steel alloy gives the camshaft strength, while the stellite on the lobe surfaces provides good wear resistance.

Lifters and Push Rods

Lifters ride on top of the camshaft lobes, transferring the "lift" of the lobe through the push rod to the rocker arm. Only solid steel or steel-hydraulic, flat-tappet, barrel-type lifters are allowed. This rule eliminates "roller lifters," which incorporate a rolling tip that rides against the cam, reducing friction and allowing much more radical lobe designs. Mushroom lifters or any lifters that assist in closing the valves are not allowed. These types of lifters are wider on the bottom than the main body of the lifter and allow the valve to open sooner and close later. This style of lifter would allow more fuel/air intake into the combustion chamber. Maximum lifter size allowed on both GM and

Valve springs must be incredibly strong to stand up to the 9,000-rpm engine speeds now common in Winston Cup racing.

Valves. There is no restriction on valve size.

Ford is limited to a .875 in. diameter. The push rods used in Winston Cup cars are a high-quality racing type, able to withstand the tremendous force within the valvetrain.

Rocker Arms

Rocker arms transfer the upward movement of the push rod into the downward movement of the valve as it opens. Rocker arms that come as standard equipment on a particular engine being used are allowed. Most teams, however, use roller-bearing rocker arms of a "split shaft" design, which are much stronger than production rocker arms.

Valve Springs

Valve springs are made from high-quality steel. As engine speeds have increased, valve springs have become difficult parts to manufacture. Winston Cup engine speeds have increased to the point where turning over 9,000 rpm is common. Harmonic problems at a particular rpm cause many valvetrain problems. Staying at an rpm to the point where bad

harmonics occurs will increase the chances of engine failure. This is especially a problem at longer tracks, where engines run a long time in 1 rpm range. Engine builders try to predict the point of bad harmonics. They then design the engine so that these areas remain in an rpm range that is not sustained for any length of time. As the engine accelerates or decelerates through this range, harmonics are usually not a problem.

Valves

Only steel and titanium valves are allowed in Winston Cup racing. There is no restriction on either intake or exhaust valve size. The valve location and the valve angle, however, must remain stock. As a practical matter, the specification of the "legal" cylinder head dictates the maximum size of the valve seats. There is very little room to increase the valve size within these parameters.

Intake Manifold

High-performance aluminum intake manifolds are used in Winston Cup racing and must be a model that has been approved by NASCAR

High-rise aluminum manifolds with individual runners for each cylinder are used.

officials. The distance from the gasket surface at the top of the manifold to the floor of the manifold "plenum" cannot exceed 6 in. The plenum is the open area inside the manifold, where the fuel/air mixture is divided into eight parts or runners, one for each cylinder.

Different intake manifold modifications can make the same engine run very differently. Epoxy fillers may be added to the individual runners to change the flow characteristics of the manifold, although fillers may not be added to the plenum floor or walls. The intake

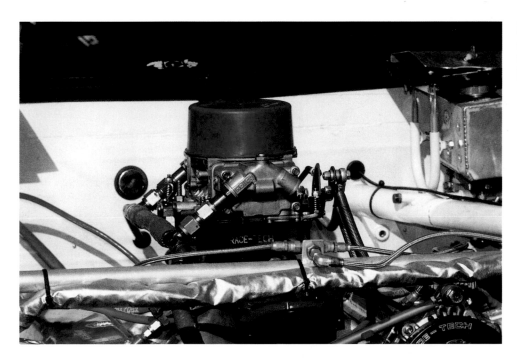

Holly 4150 series carburetors are the only ones allowed by NASCAR.

Carburetors and their use are monitored closely by racing officials. Some polishing and other minor internal changes are allowed, but no external alterations may be made. Carburetor jets must be the same type supplied by the manufacturer. Fuel injection, which is common on street cars and other forms of racing, is not allowed, although modern fuel-injection systems computers are used to manage carburetion systems. NASCAR has tried to stay away from completely computer-driven systems on the cars.

Restricter plates, mounted between the carburetor and the intake manifold, are used at Talladega and Daytona to limit the amount of fuel/air vapor to the engine. The result of this is less air, lower rpms, less horsepower, and therefore, lower speeds.

The following models are the only carburetors allowed by NASCAR:

· On all tracks except Talladega and Daytona: Holley 4150 Series with 1 9/16 in. maximum venturi and 1 11/16 in. maximum throttle bore

· At Talladega and Daytona: Holley 4150 Series with 1 3/8 in. maximum venturi and 1 11/16 in. maximum throttle bore

Air Filters

Air is brought into the engine through a cowl located at the back of the hood and in front of the windshield. All Winston Cup cars use a round, dry-type air filter, much the same as the one used on production vehicles. The mandatory minimum diameter is 14 in., and the maximum no more than 16 in. Air filter housings are made of Kevlar or metal. The top and bottom pieces must be the same diameter and must be centered on the carburetor. The air filter element must be at least 1 1/2 in. high and no more than 4 in. high. Air filters may not be removed either during the race or during practice.

Exhaust

The exhaust system on Winston Cup cars is made up of three main components: the headers, the collector pipe, and the exhaust pipes.

The headers are made from pipe, bent to a custom fit. Each pipe runs from the exhaust port on the cylinder head to the collector pipe.

A carb undergoing a rebuild.

opening size must be at least 3 9/16 in. when measured front to back, and 3 5/8 in. when measured side to side.

Carburetors

Winston Cup cars run four-barrel, mechanically advanced, secondary venturi carburetors.

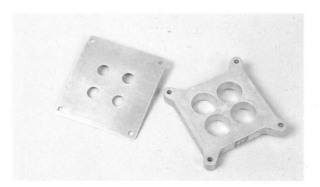

The dreaded restricter plate. The plate fits between the carburetor and the intake manifold and chokes the air supply to the motor, robbing it of power and slowing the car down.

Air filters are situated on a housing that picks up air from the rear. The air pickup is at the back of the hood at the base of the windshield.

By making each individual piece the same length, the exhaust system will help "pull" the exhaust gases from the cylinder, increasing engine efficiency. The shape, lengths, and configuration of the header pipes are adjusted to tune the powerband of the engine. This process

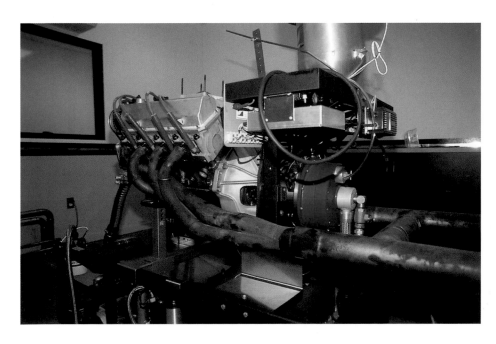

Headers and collectors (shown here on the dyno).

Teams try many exhaust configurations. Engine characteristics can be changed by altering the exhaust configuration.

allows crews to custom tailor the car's powerband to the track, building the maximum power where it is needed the most.

Collector pipes combine the four individual header runners on each side of the engine into a common pipe. Collector pipes are the links between the individual header runners and the single exhaust pipe.

Exhaust pipes begin at the collector pipe and must exit the car at the side between the

The exhaust exits the car just in front of the rear tire. There may be exhaust exiting in front of both tires or just on the left side. When the exhaust exits on the right side of the car, the exhaust pipes can become "pinched" if the car rolls too much in the turn.

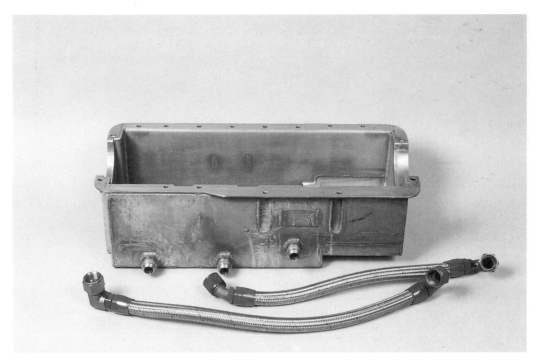

The oil pan and return lines. Unlike production cars' wet-sump oil systems, a dry-sump oil system picks the oil up from the oil pan as soon as possible and recirculates it through the oil cooler and oil tank.

front and rear wheels. They may exit the car on either side. Some teams locate both pipes on the left side of the car. This eliminates the chance that they might be pinched shut as the car pitches over in left-hand turns or makes contact with the outside wall.

Exhaust pipes may have a maximum 3 1/2 in. inside diameter and must extend past the driver, under the frame and to the outer edge of the car. They cannot be fitted into a notched area in the rocker panel, quarter panel, or frame. They must be secured to the

The oil tank may be located in the car behind the driver but must be contained in a steel box.

Breathers are located on the top of the oil tank.

car with at least two 1/8 in.-by-1 in. steel U-shaped brackets. The exhaust pipes are not round, but flattened, giving more ground clearance.

Oil System

Winston Cup cars use a dry sump oil system, a system not found on production vehicles. Instead of the oil flowing down to the pan

An oil tank that has been mounted outside the cockpit. Note the electric strip heaters that warm the oil before the race.

An extra oil-temperature gauge is used in the oil tank and located in the left side quarter window so the crew can check the temperature of the oil in the tank.

to be recycled through the engine by a pump that picks it up there, the dry sump systems keep the oil in motion at all times. The pump is mounted on the outside of the engine (much in the same manner as an alternator or power-steering pump) and is driven by a belt. After the oil runs through the engine, it is quickly "picked up" and pumped through the oil system. During circulation, the oil passes through many feet of hose, an oil tank mounted in the left rear of the car, and an oil cooler mounted in the left front of the car. The system runs at about 70–80 psi, and an acceptable range of oil temperature is 250–270 degrees F.

Oil Tank

Placed behind the driver, the oil reserve tank must be encased in a 22-gauge metal, leakproof, insulated box. The tank holds approximately 18 quarts of oil. Because of the long times that Cup engines are held at high rpms, it is necessary to run a volume of oil this high to keep it cool enough to properly lower the engine's temperature. Oil reserve tanks are always located behind the driver, putting the weight in the middle and on the inside of the car. Due to this positioning, great care is taken

The oil cooler is located behind the left front fender. This is why it is better for a car to be damaged in the right front than the left front. If the oil cooler is damaged, it will have to be replaced before the car can continue. There is also a good chance that the car will slide in its own oil and the driver will lose control.

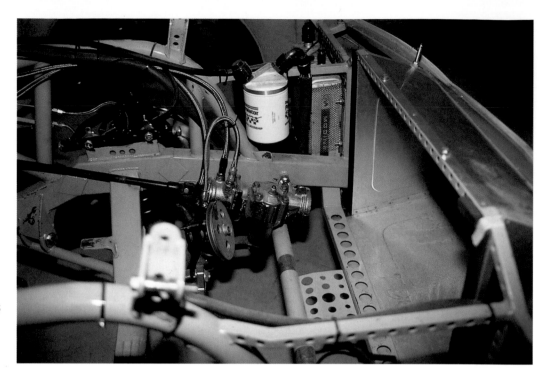

Oil filters are mounted off the engine in remote locations on Winston Cup racing cars. Their location may vary on different cars.

to make the tank and protective shield as tough as possible. An extra oil temperature gauge is located on the oil reservoir tank so that crewmen can quickly get a read on the oil temperature.

Oil Cooler

Because of modern engine speeds, proper oil cooling is essential to be competitive on the track. On Winston Cup cars, oil constantly cir-

Oil pumps get their energy from a drive belt, just like an alternator. Pumps are rebuilt after each race to ensure peak performance.

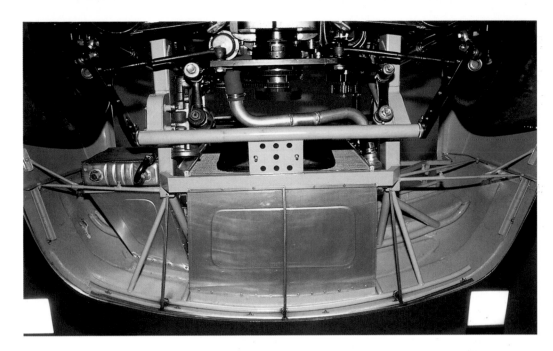

Keeping a race engine cool requires an efficient cooling system.

culates through an oil cooler (or radiator) to cool the engine temperature. As with a coolant radiator, the air (entering through the left front grill opening) is forced through the cooling fins, thereby cooling the oil that circulates through the passageways.

Mounted in the front of the car, the oil cooler is a fairly vulnerable piece of equipment. Often, a Winston Cup car cannot survive an impact to the left front, where the oil cooler is housed, that might be survivable if it were to the right front.

Oil Filters

Winston Cup cars use oil filters very much like those on production cars. Instead of being attached to the engine, though, the oil filter is mounted in the engine well at a very accessible position. Only high-quality stainless-steel braided line is used for the oil system, due to

Aluminum radiators are used.

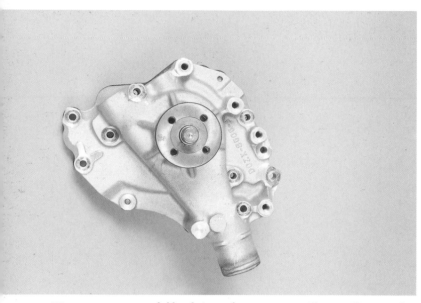

Water pumps are much like their stock counterparts. The impellers may be changed to increase the pump's efficiency.

the high temperature and the consequences of a line failure.

Oil Pumps

Winston Cup oil pumps are mounted onto the engine in much the same way an alternator is mounted. Power is transferred to the oil pump by a wide heavy-duty belt running off a special crankshaft pulley. These heavy-duty pumps have a high pumping output in order to push the oil quickly throughout the system. The oil pump may not exceed 9.5 in. in length and 3.5 in. in cross section.

Cooling System

Cooling is of critical importance to a Winston Cup engine. General requirements for Winston cup cooling systems are similar to their production counterparts but with a few modifications. No special systems that use ice, freon, or any other coolant can be used.

Electric fans are used to prevent wasting engine power by driving a fan with a belt.

Mechanical fuel pumps are still used in Winston Cup racing.

With the 14:1 compression ratings being run and the high engine speeds being turned, much more heat is generated than in a production engine. Only high-strength hoses are used in the cooling system. Lower radiator hoses are most often a one-piece metal pipe. Other hoses are braided stainless steel with special high pressure fittings. Any hose failure on the track means a hazardous wet spot for drivers to go through, so hose integrity is of prime importance.

Radiators

Winston Cup cars all use aluminum radiators that are stock appearing and mounted in the stock position but not exceeding 2 in. from vertical. Dust screens to prevent debris from entering the radiator are allowed. Overflow pipes may be relocated to the rear of the car.

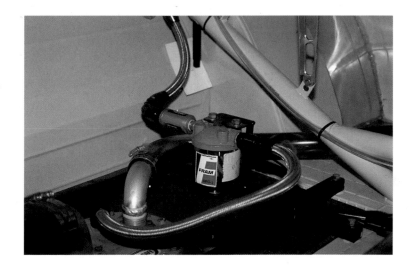

The fuel filter is mounted "inline" at the fuel cell.

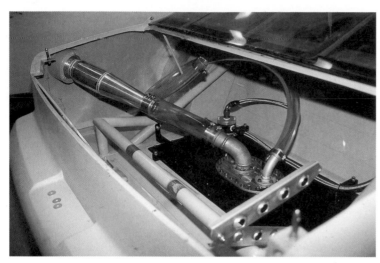

The fuel cell is mounted low in the trunk area. It is surrounded by a steel box and a tube frame.

V-type belts. Again, because of the heat generated in a Winston Cup engine, more water pump output is needed than a stock pump can provide. The impeller that does the actual pumping may be altered, changing the pitch and shape to change coolant flow rates. Changing impellers can greatly increase the pumping ability of the cooling system, and this increased circulation will improve the cooling efficiency of the entire system.

Fans

Cooling fans used in Winston Cup racing must be steel, with no fewer than four blades. The pitch of the blade is changed to increase or decrease the airflow. All fans must have at least a 14 in. diameter, and individual blades on the fan must be at least 3 1/2 in. wide. Fans must be operational and driven by a standard-type belt from the crankshaft or by an electric motor. Today, teams run electric fans that draw less energy from the engine by using a motor instead of a belt drive.

Fuel Pumps

Winston Cup cars use mechanical fuel pumps that get their pumping energy from a push rod riding on the camshaft. For safety reasons, electric fuel pumps are not allowed in Winston Cup racing. If an engine with a mechanical pump quits running, the fuel quits pumping. However, in a car with an electric fuel

One of the biggest problems with radiators is clogging as a result of small pieces of tire rubber ground off the cars during racing. These small, gooey pieces become stuck inside the fins of the radiator, impairing its ability to pass air and cool the fluids. This is why the dust screens are cleaned during pit stops.

Water Pumps

Most Winston Cup cars run with specially built, custom-made water pumps, although they must be driven with standard production

Winston Cup cars use high-performance after-market ignition systems. Two separate units are installed, so if one breaks, the driver can switch to the backup system without pitting.

pump, the fuel may keep pumping even if the engine quits running. In a crash situation this could be disastrous, as raw fuel continuing to be pumped over a hot engine may ignite.

High-quality stainless-steel braided fuel line is used. Braided stainless line is rated to a much higher pressure than regular fuel line, and is much more resistant to damage and wear.

Fuel Cell

Instead of a regular production gas tank, Winston Cup cars are required to use a "fuel cell." Fuel cells have a plastic body much stronger than a stock tank and are much harder to damage. They are partitioned so that, in the event of a rupture, fuel will not gush out of the opening. The fuel cell is encased in a 22-gauge steel fuel-cell container. They are located in the trunk, along the centerline of the car, placed as far forward as possible. The fuel-cell container is also encased in a steel frame assembly for more strength. The fuel pickup lines may be placed on the right or left side (or both) of the fuel cell. The filler for the fuel cell is located on the left quarter panel. The filler neck inside diameter may not exceed 2.125 in. A 1.25 in. inside diameter vent/overflow tube is mandatory.

Ignition

Distributors are mounted in the stock location and maintain the firing order of the stock

Alternators remain pretty much in their stock position.

model being raced. High-quality after-market distributors and plug wires—which outperform their stock counterparts—are used. Only analog systems are permitted—no programmable or computerized systems are allowed.

The major ignition system components are located in the cockpit, to the right of the driver. This protects the equipment from debris and heat. All cars have two separate ignition systems, each controlling one of two coils mounted side by side. In the event of an ignition failure, the driver can quickly flip a switch, changing to the backup system without having to make a pit stop.

The battery is located in a space in front of the left rear fender well.

High-quality after-market starters are used.

Alternator

All cars have a functioning alternator that must work within preset specifications. Only standard V-type drive belts are allowed.

Battery

The battery is located in a box mounted behind the driver in order to keep the weight on the left side and in the center of the car. The compartment is accessed through a door in the front of the left rear wheelwell. A standard high-quality 12-volt battery is used.

Starters

Winston Cup cars must be able to start under their own power, meaning that they must all have working starters. After a race is under way, a car may be "push started" in the pits, but a car can never be pushed onto the track during the race.

THE DRIVETRAIN

Multidisc clutch and flywheel.

Winston Cup cars use after-market four-speed manual transmissions. Most of these have straight-cut gears and can be shifted without using the clutch.

Flywheel

Flywheels must be solid and made of steel. The starter ring size must be the same size as the production starter ring gear. Drilling holes to lighten them is not allowed.

Clutch

Multiple-disc clutches are permitted in Winston Cup racing. The clutch housing assembly or cover can be aluminum or steel, and the pressure plates and discs must be steel. The minimum clutch diameter allowed is 7.25 in. Most teams use a three- or four-disc system with small-diameter discs. Even though the discs are smaller than those in stock clutches, these multidisc clutches have much more surface area, allowing them to stand up to the extreme strains of a 700-plus horsepower engine. Longer tracks can be hard on clutches, mainly when the car leaves the pits. Due to the rear gear ratios needed to reach the higher speeds of super speedways, starting in first gear from a dead stop is like starting in second or third gear in a street car.

Teams may use only special clutch housings that are stronger than stock parts. A 3/8 in. steel scatter-shield, an important piece of equipment, is mandatory. At the high rpms that the engines turn, a broken clutch component or flywheel can become a very dangerous

The transmission mounted in the car.

The driveshaft must be painted white, so if it comes loose, it will be visible on the racetrack.

projectile—dangerous not only to the driver but also the other drivers on the track. The scatter-shield works to contain any breakaway components, preventing them from being released to do damage.

Transmission

Winston Cup cars use special after-market four-speed transmissions, and all forward and reverse gears must be operational. If a gear in the transmission fails after the race begins, the car may continue racing. No automatic or semiautomatic transmissions are allowed.

Driveshaft

Driveshafts must be similar in design to standard production types. Two steel brackets are placed around the driveshaft and attached to the floor or cross member, preventing the driveshaft from dropping to the track in case of failure. Driveshafts must be painted white, so if the brackets fail, the driveshaft can be seen by other drivers and the race spotters.

Rear End

Different tracks require different rear-end gear ratios to ensure that all engine power available is optimized. An example of a rear gear ratio is 4.11 to 1 (or 4.11:1). This means that the drive shaft turns 4.11 revolutions for every 1 revolution of the tire.

REAR GEAR RATIOS BY TRACK

The following are the approximate rear gear ratios run at various tracks.

Atlanta	3.64:1
Bristol	5.25:1
Charlotte	3.70:1
Darlington	3.90:1
Daytona	2.94:1
Dover Downs	4.11:1
Indianapolis	4.20:1
Martinsville	6.20:1
Michigan	3.70:1
New Hampshire	3.60:1
North Carolina (Rockingham)	4.22:1
Phoenix	4.22:1
Pocono	3.89:1
Richmond	4.86:1
Sears Point	5.30:1
Talladega	2.94:1
Watkins Glen	3.89:1

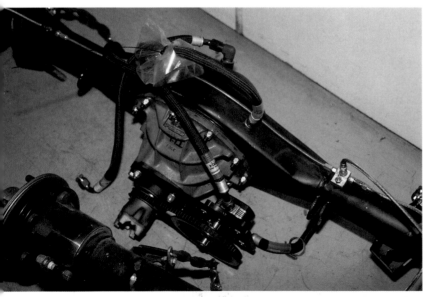

A large number of rear ends is a necessity, with ratios ranging from 2.90 to 6.11. Shown here is the rear axle assembly. While most forms of racing use an independent rear, Cup cars still run a solid axle. Note the pump with the drive belt assembly. The rear gear oil is circulated and cooled to help prevent gear failure.

The steering wheel and steering column. Note the center hub padding on the steering wheel and the additional padding on the column. The radio activation button is also visible. The driver depresses this button to speak to the crew.

Few things in Winston Cup racing are as important as a properly tuned suspension. How the individual suspension components are adjusted determines the "suspension setup." These setups are the difference between cars that handle well and cars that don't. It is important to remember that horsepower will get you down the straights faster, but the winning race car is usually the one that gets through the corners the fastest. Setups are discussed further in Chapter Four.

STEERING

Steering Wheel
All Winston Cup cars must use a steering wheel with steel spokes supporting the rim. The wheels have a "quick-release system." These

quick-release systems make it easier for a driver to get into and out of the car, and are especially critical after a crash. The wheel diameter is determined by the driver, who chooses the wheel size that gives him the best "feel" when driving the car. Steering wheels are marked so the driver knows when the wheels are pointed exactly forward. Because of the tight fit between fender and tire, the tires will not come

The steering wheel must be removed for the driver to be able to enter the car.

The steering gear and lower steering column and pitman arm during the assembly process. As the column rotates, the gear changes the motion from a circular one to the back-and-forth motion of the pitman arm.

off during pit stops if the wheels are not straightforward.

Steering Columns

Steering columns are made of steel. The center top of the steering post must have 2 in. of resilient material. A collapsible section must be made into the steering shaft for safety in the event of heavy front impact. Any universal joints used in the steering column, along with the collapsible section of the shaft, must be acceptable to racing officials.

Steering Gear

A "worm-type" gear is used in the steering system. A power steering pump assists the driver

The front suspension.

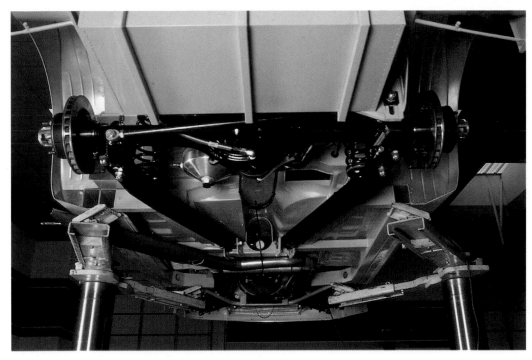

The rear suspension.

in turning the car (without power steering, you might as well add another "0" to a 500 mile race!). When the steering wheel is turned, it transfers the circular motion of the steering wheel through the steering shaft to the steering gear. One end of the steering gear is attached to the Pittman arm, which changes the circular motion of the wheel into lateral motion. The other end of the Pittman arm is attached to the centerlink. As the centerlink moves back and forth, the motion is transferred through tie rods to the steering knuckles, on which the front wheels are mounted. The idler arm, also attached to the centerlink, is used to stabilize the centerlink's movement.

Coil Springs

Winston Cup cars use coil springs made of heavy-duty steel on both the front and rear suspensions. Springs must have a minimum

A front coil spring is fit between the frame and lower control arms. The upper spring fixture is fitted with a large threaded bolt, allows for wedge adjustments to be made. The hood must be up to make front wedge adjustments.

The rear wedge is adjusted just like the front. The wedges can be taken care of quickly by accessing the bolt through a tube that extends upward through the read glass.

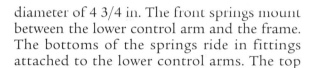

The rear coil spring. The bottom of the spring fits into the trailing arm. The top rides in a fixture under the chassis.

diameter of 4 3/4 in. The front springs mount between the lower control arm and the frame. The bottoms of the springs ride in fittings attached to the lower control arms. The top spring mounts are welded to the frame rails. On the rear suspension, the upper and lower coil spring mounts must be located between the rear frame side rails. The rear lower mounts must be located on either the rear axle trailing arms or on top of the rear axle housing. The upper mounts must be welded to the chassis directly above the lower mounts.

The top of the front shock is attached to the frame and the bottom onto the lower control arm.

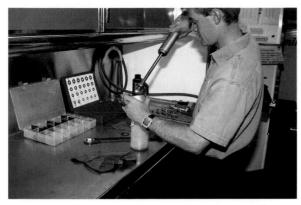

Shocks are rebuilt after every race. It is also possible for teams to change components in the shocks to fine-tune them.

Springs are categorized by spring rates, which is the resistance a spring exerts when compressed, measured in pounds of force. Because of the importance of springs in making a car handle well, crews will test many combinations of spring rates on various corners of the car. On all tracks except road courses, a setup will have a different spring rate at each corner of the car to counter the particular forces that track applies to the car as it turns. Special openings go through the rear window to allow the rear jack bolts to be turned very quickly during pit stops. The hood, however, must be opened to adjust the front springs. Rubber inserts are allowed between the spring coils to add stiffness to the spring.

Even after the team finds the right combination, its work is not done. Winston Cup cars are built with fixtures on the upper spring mount that allow teams to tune spring rates even finer. These devices are known as jack bolts or jack screws. As they are tightened or loosened, they increase or decrease the spring rate, which is usually called "putting wedge in the car" or simply "adjusting the wedge." Fans will see this done during pit stops.

Shocks

Winston Cup cars use heavy-duty shocks similar to the original shocks on the models being raced, and they are required to be available to all competitors.

The top of the rear shock is attached to the frame and the bottom to the trailing arm.

Some say that as much time is spent figuring out what shocks to run as is spent on the rest of the setup process combined. Only one shock per wheel is allowed, and placing the shocks in the middle of the coil springs is not allowed. How the car handles through the turns depends greatly on the shock being used. Because of this, shock absorbers are tuned just like most other parts of the car. A "shock dyno" is used to test the shock rebound and handling characteristics. Teams can fine-tune the shock at the shop and the track to achieve the combination they desire.

Sway Bars

Steel sway bars link the suspension and the chassis/body together. The stiffer the sway bar, the tighter the link between the chassis and the

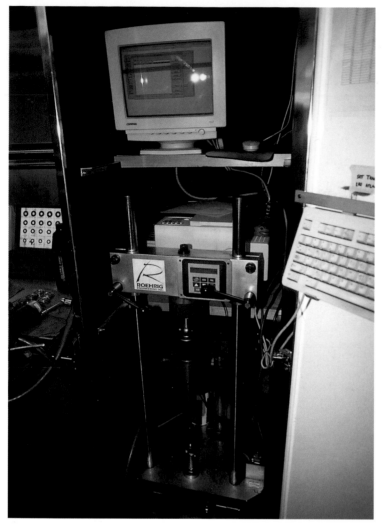

The shock dyno tests the shocks to ensure that they are operating properly. They are a myriad of adjustments settings for the different tracks.

suspension. The tighter the link, the less movement between the suspension and the chassis, resulting in less "body roll" when the car is turning. If the sway bars are too stiff, however, control problems may result. Teams have many sway bar strengths available to allow them to tune the body roll to fit the track being raced.

Steering Knuckles

Steering knuckles link the suspension and steering systems to the wheel. The upper and lower control arms are attached to the knuckle with ball-joints. The wheel bearings ride on the spindle located on the outside of the knuckle.

Control Arms

Control arms are the main link between the chassis and the front suspension. The inside of the upper control arms is mounted to the frame using pivoting mounts with heavy-duty bushings, and to the steering knuckles on the outside using ball-joints. The lower control arms attach to the frame and the steering knuckles. The front coil spring lower mounts are found on the lower control arms. Winston Cup cars use specially manufactured tubular control arms that are much lighter and stronger than their stock counterparts.

Trailing Arms

Trailing arms link the chassis and the rear suspension. The fronts of the trailing arms attach to the body with hinged fixtures just aft of the center of the car. The backs of the trailing arms attach to the rear axle and have fixtures to connect the rear shock absorbers and the rear springs, which run from the frame to the trailing arms.

Track Bar

The track bar is used to adjust the roll center of the car and to keep the rear end "square" under the car. As the car goes through the turn, the rear end will be twisted in relation to the body. Track or "panhard" bars are attached at one end to the frame and at the other end to the end of one of the trailing arms. Usually the bar

The sway bar setup. The center bar is clamped into the outer ends by a splined fitting. They are in turn connected to the trailing arm in the back and the lower control arm in the front.

Many sizes of sway bars are available to the teams. The bigger the bar, the stiffer the suspension/ body connection, and the less body roll the car will have in the turns.

runs from the left side of the body to the right rear trailing arm. This extra support is critical for stability through the turns. The track bar can be adjusted to refine the handling of the car during both practice and the race.

WHEELS AND TIRES

Winston Cup cars run 9.5 in. x 15 in. steel wheels and specially produced racing tires. Currently, all Winston Cup tires are supplied by Goodyear. These race tires are a radial design and made of a

The steering knuckle and front bearing assembly being fitted onto a car.

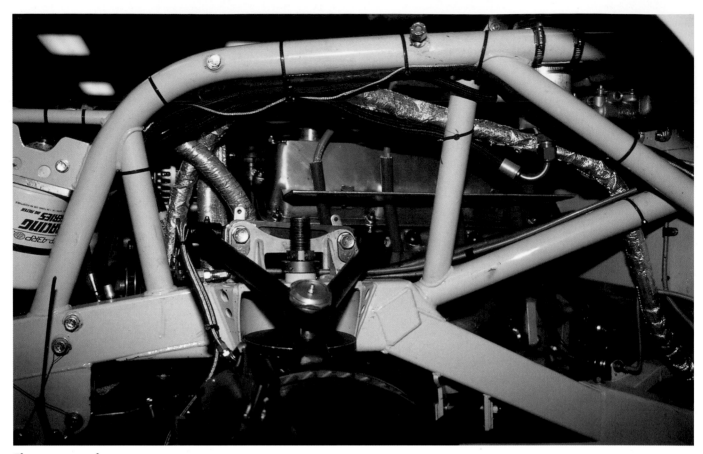

The upper control arm.

much softer rubber than even the most radical performance street tires. They have no tread pattern because they are intended to be used only in dry conditions. Tires cannot exceed 13.2 in. of sidewall height at 60 psi of air pressure.

The friction between the racing surface and the tire heats the rubber, making it even softer. It is this soft rubber and the tires' heavy sidewall construction that allow the cars to achieve such high speeds in the turns. While the car is

The upper control arm mounting point. Note the inserts, which can be changed to adjust the angle of the control arm, which affects the handling of the car.

The lower control arm.

on the track, rubber cakes up in the engine well and on the underside of the hood. After a short track race there may be pounds of shredded rubber all over the car.

Tire wear differs depending on the type of track being raced. For safety reasons, tires incor-porate an inner-liner—a small heavy-duty inner tube mounted on the rim inside the racing tire. In the case of a blowout, this inner-liner is supposed to keep the rim from digging into the pavement and causing the car to flip. At over a thousand dollars a set, a team's tire bill can be staggering!

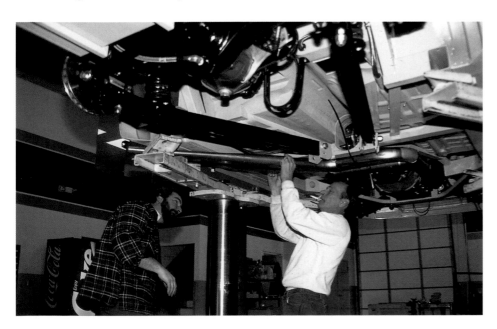

The trailing arms support the rear suspension and are attached to the frame. Winston Cup cars run very long trailing arms for smooth handling.

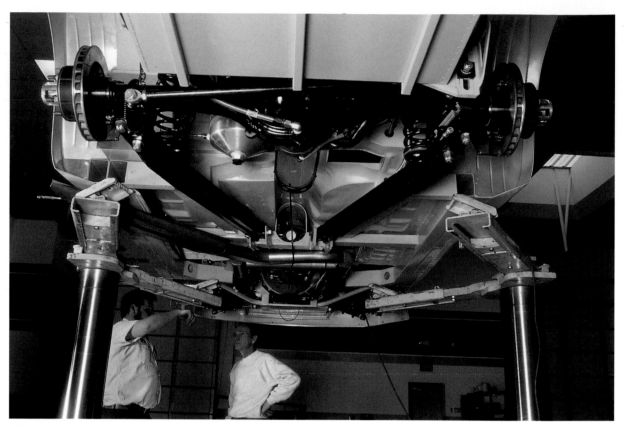

The track bar runs from the trailing arm to the body.

A "scuff" tire is a tire that has been run for a few laps to "work the tire in." Depending on the track conditions and the setup of the car, teams may scuff new tires during practice to prepare them for use in the race. "Sticker" tires are new, unused tires that still have the Goodyear factory sticker on them.

The track bar adjustment point. As the bolt is turned the bar can be raised or lowered.

Brand-new Goodyear "sticker tires."

BRAKES

Master Cylinders

Master cylinders on Winston Cup cars are a simple, non-power-assisted type that are mounted on the driver-side firewall in roughly the same location as in production cars.

Brake Lines

Brake lines must be much stronger than their street counterparts. On short tracks, road courses, and some longer tracks, the demand on the brakes becomes critical. The heat generated at the rotor/pad contact dissipates through the caliper and into the fluid. The fluid, in turn, heats the brake lines. When subjected to such heat, production brake lines become weak, and the pressure of applying the brakes will cause them to swell. This decreases the pressure at the pad and makes entire the brake system less efficient. The strength of braided stainless-steel lines helps to overcome this problem.

Calipers

Brake calipers respond to the pressure created by pressing the brake pedal and squeeze the brake pads against the rotor. This is accomplished by the pressure from the master cylinder being transmitted through the brake line to the caliper. At the caliper, the brake fluid presses against pistons, which press against the brake pads, slowing the car down. Most street car calipers have one or two pistons per caliper,

Scuff tires have been put on the car and run for a few laps to roughen them up.

Goodyear race tires have much softer rubber than street tires. This gives the cars tremendous grip. Rubber from the tires is visible on the hood after a practice run.

Brake cooling is essential on short tracks and road courses. The air is picked up through the grill and ducted directly onto the brakes.

Non-vacuum-assisted master cylinders are mounted in the stock position on the firewall.

while Winston Cup calipers have four pistons per caliper, allowing more pressure to be applied to the pads. Racing calipers must be built to stand up to the incredible heat generated when braking hard.

Brake Pads

Brake pads are made especially for the purpose of racing. Due to the extreme heat encountered in racing brakes, normal street pads would wear out far too quickly. Instead of being made predominantly of an organic material, racing pads are a carbon/metal mix, which is much more heat- and wear-resistant.

Rotors

Rotors used in Winston Cup racing must be made of steel and be able to stand up to extreme heat for long periods of time. Brake rotors will continue to work up to approximately 1,200 degrees. At about this temperature they begin to glow. This can be seen at night races at Bristol as the cars brake before entering the turn. If the temperature continues

High-quality braided-steel brake lines are used. These hoses stand up to high temperatures much better than stock rubber hose does.

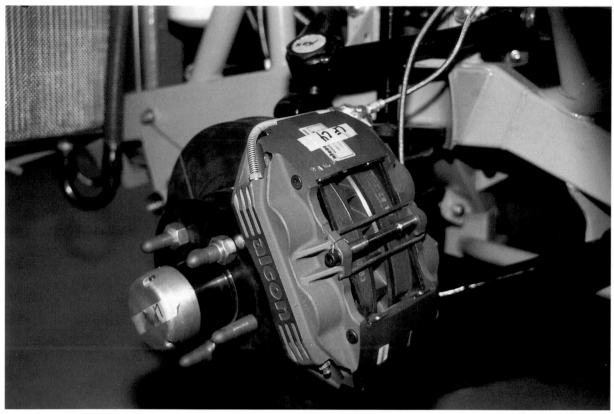

After-market calipers are used. They have four pistons per caliper, whereas most stock calipers have one or two pistons per caliper.

to rise, the heat is transferred into the caliper. When this happens the brake fluid will begin to boil, releasing air into the brake system. A driver will "lose" the pedal when air contaminates the system. Air released into the hydraulic brake system will result in the pedal going all the way to the floor when it is depressed.

At some tracks, Talladega or Daytona, for example, brake overheating is not a problem as brakes are seldom used other than during pit stops. However, at tracks like Bristol or Martinsville, keeping the brakes cool is one of

Brake pads fitted into the caliper. A 500-lap short-track race is about the life span of a set of pads.

Thick rotors with vented discs are used on tracks where there is a premium on braking.

the most critical problems the teams must address. While all the components making up the braking system are of the highest quality, they must still be cooled to work efficiently. This cooling is accomplished by ducting air through openings in the body onto the brake components.

Cars may have a maximum of three air scoops per brake. Each scoop directs air to the brakes with flexible hose (with a maximum diameter of 3 in.). A 24-square-inch maximum scoop size is allowed. The scoops cannot extend forward of the leading edge of the air dam. Headlight openings may also be used for brake cooling. Fans or blowers may be used to increase the airflow to the brakes, although liquid cooling of the brakes, which is used in some forms of auto racing, is not permitted.

On super speedways, where braking is necessary only when pitting, a lighter rotor with holes drilled in the discs are used.

New cars must be built before the season starts. It's best to have six or eight full assembled race cars before the first race. More will be built—and rebuilt—throughout the racing season.

THE TEAMS

Winston Cup racing is a team sport—to be successful in Winston Cup racing you must have a fast car, a good driver, and a well-tuned crew (easier said than done). Saying that one person on the team is more important than another is like trying to determine which is more important to your life—your brain, heart, or lungs. Even if you have the best of one of these, you won't last long if you don't have the other two. Likewise, the best driver in the world may take 20 laps to gain track position only to lose it because of one extra second during a pit stop.

If you watch racing, you know how valuable those 17-second pit stops are in terms of track position. Consider a yellow flag pit stop in a race where a number of cars are a lap down. Coming out of the pits in first place or seventh place means 13 cars to pass to get to the lead. Late in a race, this can be the difference in winning or not.

NASCAR teams do much more than just what is seen during pit stops. Taking four tires off, putting four tires on, filling the car with fuel, adjusting the chassis, cleaning the air

The hood and paint scheme go to the primary sponsor. Prices typically run from $5 to 10 million.

intakes, cleaning the windshield, and giving the driver whatever he needs in 17 to 18 seconds is only part of the job. Long before the season starts teams are hard at work.

To put a team together, an owner or manager must not only assemble an experienced, compatible racing team; he must also have a sound business plan. Getting started can be difficult for new teams. The main source of funding for a Winston Cup team is the sponsor. Without a sponsor, it is hard to last long on the circuit. Securing full sponsorship can be somewhat like the chicken and the egg. To get a sponsor who will supply the money, a team must be competitive. But in order to be competitive a team must have money. It's common to see cars in a race with no sponsorship. This is a gamble an owner must take, betting that his car will run well enough to catch the eye of a potential sponsor.

The amount of money a team charges a sponsor varies. Typically, the better the team, the more air time they will get, and the more they can charge. Usually, the primary sponsor will pay $5–10 million a year. However, there

The window pillar behind the driver will go for $100,000 to $200,000.

are a few teams running that supposedly receive as much as $10–13 million a year.

Sponsors pay to be seen, and the hood is the primary spot for a sponsor to place its decals. The paint scheme will also reflect the primary sponsor's corporate image. In cases where a team may have one or more associate sponsors, these companies will be represented by smaller stickers on the car in less-prominent places. Usually the position of the sticker determines the price. The pillar directly behind the side window will probably cost an associate sponsor $100,000–200,000. The area behind the quarter window, $200,000–400,000. The

Deck lids go for around half a million dollars.

The quarter panel will cost $700,000 to $800,000.

deck lid area will run around a half-million; lower quarter panel (in front of the rear tire) $400,000–600,000. Behind the rear tire on the quarter panel will cost around $700,000 or $800,000. And the area on the back of the car, under the spoiler, will go for a million or more. These prices are influenced by the amount of air time each spot gets. For instance, the area under the spoiler is often seen on camera, therefore a team can ask a higher price than for

The lower quarter panel around the rear tire runs about half a million dollars.

The area under the spoiler goes for around a million.

an area of the car not seen as much on camera.

Once the owner has secured sponsorship or has enough money to race the car until one is found, it's time to start working. The owner must assemble the team, realizing that the way the team and driver mesh is one of the most important factors for winning. New chassis and engines must be built, rented, or bought and then tested. Because teams are limited in the amount of testing they can do

During testing, teams are allowed to use computers and other equipment not allowed during the race weekend itself. Here, testing equipment is hooked to the car before it leaves to test at Indy.

at the track, the testing that is done is critical.

From testing bodies in the wind tunnel to engines on the dyno, a great deal of research must be done. Supplier relationships are also critical, and not just because of the necessity of being able to get dependable racing parts. The knowledge of the supplier helps solve problems that arise as cars are made to go faster and faster, with engines turning ever-increasing rpms.

Once an owner has assembled the sponsor, parts, and people, his job is far from over. The team must have a shop with all the tools that it needs to work with. As the sponsor's role in Winston Cup racing has grown, so have the standards for all the equipment used by the team. While a team is made up of professionals

From a fabrication point of view, the car builders' efforts result in racing masterpieces. Not only are they very rugged, reliable, and fast; they also have aggressive good looks.

Mechanics are everywhere. General mechanics install the cars' systems. Every system of the car demands the ultimate in detail, and every part of the car has a designated specialist.

The body and paint men refurbish the cars between races. They repair damage, strip the car clean, and paint it. Not only are these vehicles race cars, they are also multimillion-dollar 200 mph billboards.

who understand the dynamics of a race car, they also have another responsibility: They represent the company that sponsors the car. Everything from the shop to the car, haulers to uniforms, must be clean and attractive.

When the season finally starts, there is still more for the owner to do. Transportation must be arranged for the team and equipment for all 32 races and all test sessions. Hotel reservations, parking permits, track credentials, airfare, coordination of the sponsor's activities at the track, down to small details such as having the driver's and the team members' medical histories on hand in case of an accident. The importance of these arrangements cannot be overstated. If a team has logistics problems, the members' minds may not be 100 percent on racing, and the team's performance could suffer.

A race car will not win on the ability of the driver alone. Many things must be done correctly to give the driver the chance to show his ability. The winner is not always the team with the smartest people or the most money. Winning often is the product of endless compromise between team members. Ideas are presented, discussed, and then implemented. It is this ability to communicate and work together that often results in a winning race car.

Skilled machinists are a must. Today's shops use sophisticated computerized machining centers.

Before leaving for the track, the chassis specialist will take great care in installing the appropriate suspension setup under the car. Once the team gets the car to the track, however, they will change it.

The nature of racing places intense demands on the teams. In any given race, only one out of 42 or 43 teams will win. The others may spend a great deal of time and money only to tear up a race car, be it their fault or someone else's. Under all this pressure, combined with being on the road some 35 weeks a year, the modern team must have stamina as well as skill.

The task of fielding a winning race car has become so complex that it takes many people to compete. This extends from the person selling sponsorships on the car to the driver on the track. Many things have to happen just to get the car to the track.

While all teams are set up differently, the following pages show general team job descriptions and responsibilities.

TEAM MANAGER

Most teams designate one person to be team manager. The manager's primary responsibilities involve the business and logistics of the team, including day-to-day administrative duties such as overseeing the accounting functions, and making sure bills are paid and the payroll is met. Team managers usually oversee the personnel functions of a race team, including hiring, dismissal, and salary distribution. The manager must also address the long-range plans for the team and take part in the marketing decisions.

CREW CHIEF

All Winston Cup teams have a crew chief, who is usually responsible for all things related to the technical aspects of the race car and the crew. This includes car preparation at the shop and at the track. Simply put, the crew chief's job is to make sure everything gets done and gets done properly. In Winston Cup racing the buck stops with the crew chief.

At the track, crew members must learn to work in very tight quarters.

The track changes during the race, and as the car accumulates miles, the handling characteristics of the car change. One of the crew chief's primary jobs during practice and during the race is to communicate with the driver and try to understand and interpret his comments and descriptions on how the car is handling. He must evaluate suggestions from the crew and driver and decide what changes and adjustments are needed to make the car faster. If the car is running well, he decides how to maintain the existing handling characteristics. This ability to diagnose and adjust is one of the main ingredients in creating a winning race team.

CHASSIS SPECIALIST

The chassis specialist is responsible for all things related to the car in terms of body setup and suspension setup. Long before the season starts, the chassis specialist is hard at work preparing the stable of cars necessary to run a Winston Cup team. The frames and roll cages must be built or purchased, and then the bodies must be put on the car. Teams may buy assembled cars, though many teams choose to make their own chassis and bodies. As the cars are assembled, they must be tested on the track and in the wind tunnel. Teams build different cars for different types of

While racing at NASCAR's highest level can be glamorous, much of the work can be monotonous. For every race and practice session the gear must be loaded into the hauler at the shop, unloaded to the garage at the track, moved to the pits for the race, reloaded into the truck after the race, and finally unloaded back at the shop (quickly, so the truck can be reloaded before the next race).

tracks (speedways, short tracks, and road courses). Chassis specialists must be able to understand the variety of tracks and be able to build cars for every category, refining a particular car to a particular track.

The owner or team manager is always busy at the track. The owner of five teams, Jack Rousch is still a hands-on member of each one.

The buck stops with the crew chief. He is responsible for all things related to the race car. As a result crew chiefs are usually all over the car, involved in all decisions being made about the setup. This is why Ray Evernham is considered by many to be the best in the business.

ENGINE SPECIALIST

The engine specialist is responsible for the preparation of the engines at the shop, during the race setup, and during the race. He is also responsible for the rebuilding of the engines between races. A number of engines will be prepared at the shop before heading out to the track. These engines will have been run on the dyno to ensure that they are building enough power and that the power comes on in the right rpm range for the track on which they will race. When the teams swap engines at the track, the new engine is usually ready to be run immediately. This advanced engine preparation is what makes it possible for teams to blow an engine at the end of practice Saturday and still be able to race competitively on Sunday with an engine that has not yet been run on the track.

Engine builders must evaluate similar components and decide which is best to use. Many hours of testing and retesting are required to make a sound decision. Engine builders must constantly look for the small changes that can be made to gain a quarter of a horsepower here

Bill Elliott's crew chief, Mike Beam, along with his crew, pushes the Elliot-driven Ford Taurus to the starting grid.

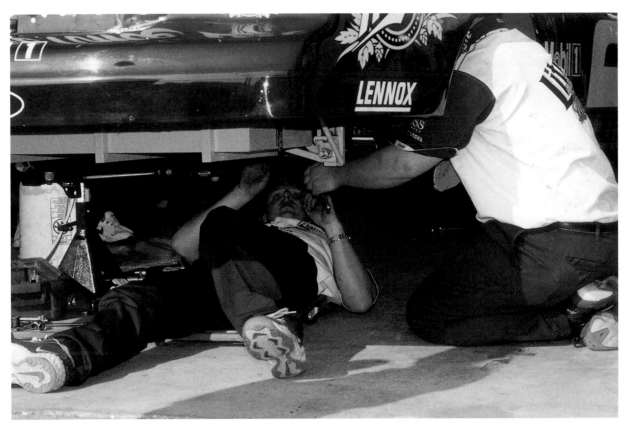

The typical view of the chassis specialist during the race weekend. Crews try many suspension combinations during the practice sessions before the race.

and half a horsepower there. Good engine builders know that enough of these small refinements, when accumulated, give an advantage on the track.

PUBLIC RELATIONS MANAGER

As Winston Cup racing has grown and sponsorships have come to play such an important role, most teams now have a public relations manager. Like any other product, a race team must be properly marketed. The public relations manager coordinates the sponsor with the race team to make sure that the needs of both are met.

Show car schedules must be arranged, and when sponsors have special events at races, the public relations manager must ensure that the

sponsors and their guests have the full "racing experience." These activities, however, must not be allowed to distract the crews. While supporting the sponsor-team relationship, the public relations manager must also coordinate

Springs, shocks, sway bars, control arms, and a host of other parts must be swapped out quickly if teams are to get the most out of the practice sessions. Here, some crew members swap motors while others attend to the suspension.

The engine specialist is constantly tuning and monitoring the motor during practice. The motor must build power at the right time. Everything from manifolds to rear gear may be changed to adjust the motor. In this photo, the timing is being checked.

Public relations managers must promote their drivers and teams in the media. Some drivers enjoy this portion of their job more than other drivers do.

The spotters on race day. On large tracks and road courses, more than one spotter may be used.

all the media-related activities, from setting up driver appearances to supplying reporters and newspapers with information. The public relations manager is constantly striving to put the team and its sponsor into the spotlight.

SPOTTER

The spotter is the driver's and crew's extra set of eyes. Constantly watching the track, the spotter alerts the driver to situations on the track ahead of the driver's vision. Spotters warn of

The pit crew must perform like a well-tuned machine. A miscue here means losing valuable track position.

Strength and dexterity are necessary to be a jack man. The jack man must also watch the tire changers so he doesn't drop the car off the jack before they are finished. All of this can be difficult when surrounded by the rest of the crew.

accidents, slower traffic, and pursuing cars. Spotters may also note how a competitor's car is handling on the track and may offer suggestions on passing techniques based on these observations. They may also watch the line the faster cars are running and feed this information back to the driver. On larger tracks, more than one spotter may be used, with each spotter concentrating on one particular part of the track.

Tire specialists monitor the tire wear, pressure, and temperature, which are critical in adjusting the suspension.

Tire changers must always have a flawless motion. They practice a great deal to be as fast and precise as they are. If their rhythm is broken they will cost the team valuable seconds.

JACK MAN

The jack man must have strength, dexterity, and a very keen eye. The jack man must be quick enough to run around the car and all the other team members to place the jack. The jack man must also watch both tire changers to ensure that the tires are properly changed before he drops the car. If he drops it too soon, the resulting delay would be substantial, as the car must be rejacked before the problem can be corrected. This one scenario has cost the race for many teams.

TIRE SPECIALIST

The tire specialist is responsible for the preparation of the tires. Many times, the tire setup is changed during pit stops. For this to take place, the tires must be carefully prepared and analyzed. Tire pressure, rubber condition, and stagger are all involved in fine-tuning the car's handling characteristics. The crew chief must be able to rely on the tire specialist to provide the tires specifically called for in the desired setup.

The gas man must be strong and agile. He must handle a can of gas that, when full, weighs more than 70 pounds.

GAS MAN

As with the jack man, strength and dexterity are required here. The physical aspects of the job are demanding. The gas man must climb over the pit wall, carrying the full gas can. Eleven gallons at roughly 6 lb each makes for

The catch-can man catches the gas overflow in a can, for safety reasons. If the overflow gas is not contained, a fire would start much easier.

an ungainly 70 lb or so. A gas man must carry the can high so the fill nozzle can be immediately connected when he reaches the car. This eliminates any extra time required to lift the can to the car.

CATCH-CAN MAN

As the fuel flows into the fuel cell during the fueling process, the air in the fuel cell escapes through a vent hose, which exits at the left rear of the deck lid. As the tank becomes full, fuel will escape up through this vent tube as well. The catch-can man's job is to ensure that no gas escaping from this vent sprays fuel where it could ignite. This job was added after fuel overflow caused a number of fires during pit stops. The catch-can man can also assist the gas man in supporting the fill tank.

Once the race starts, the crews and the fans have the same job. If the car is running well, everyone is pretty much spectators until the pit stops. Racing can be much like the Army. Hurry up and wait.

CHAPTER 3

During the off-season, many cars must be built in preparation for the upcoming year. Cars will be damaged or totally destroyed, and the team must stay ahead of the game and not run out.

THE SHOPS

SECTION 3.1 — THE SHOP AND EQUIPMENT

To build winning cars, a Winston Cup team must have a shop equipped with all the tools needed to build, prepare, and maintain the cars. Building today's race cars takes much more than just bolting the pieces together. Specialized equipment and talent are needed to attain the excellence required for today's competitive racing. The shops have changed dramatically in the last decade, many of the more recent ones being built more to resemble sites of Fortune 500 companies than garages. Not only have shops become large but they have also become plush. So much of racing has become image-oriented that it has affected how the shops look. As the sponsor's role has grown, so has the need for everything

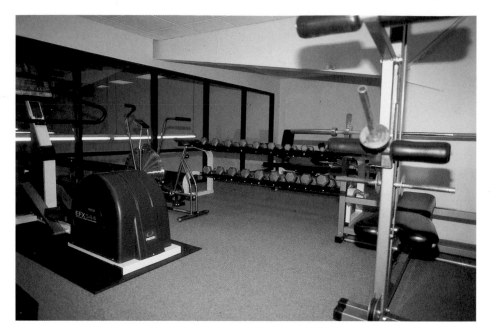

Physical fitness has become important in Winston Cup racing for both driver and crew, so fitness centers are now standard in modern race shops. With the importance of pit stop speed, only the most fit now have the over-the-wall (pit crew) jobs.

associated with the team to be first class. With the popularity of the sport growing, more interviews and technical clips shown during the race take place at the shop. A well-equipped, nicely designed shop also has a positive effect on the team. A perfect workplace has an effect on attitude, and attitude has a great deal to do with winning.

Storage space is essential. From chemicals to cylinder heads, extras of everything must be kept on hand. This can add up into quite a bit of square footage.

Teams must keep a large stable of cars, given all the different types of tracks run. Most competitive teams have around a dozen in some state of completion. Lots of work space is required. If everyone is running into each other, they can't work efficiently.

CNC (computer numerically controlled) machining equipment is used. This type of equipment can be programmed to machine a part a specific way. While this equipment is very expensive, it does ensure repeatability and consistency. Yet even with this type of equipment, a great deal of finishing work is still done by hand.

Every shop has a graveyard. There are always a few cars that you don't want to sell, but they are too broken or too old to rebuild.

Mills and lathes are necessary for the many machining jobs that must be done. Here, a camshaft is in the process of being made ready to run. Very few products go out of the box and onto the car without some type of modification.

The primary assembly area. This is where the chassis and body are assembled.

The shop must have surface plates. These steel plates are level and true and allow the teams to work on the car knowing that it is on a very flat surface.

The cars seem to go on forever. A team must have many different types of cars. Super-speedway cars, intermediate-track cars, short-track cars, and road-course cars must all be made.

The sheet-metal fabrication room. This is where the body panels are made.

A chassis is ready for a new life. After being damaged, it was stripped, cleaned, and will be painted and rebuilt into a new race car.

The engine assembly room. Everything is kept as clean and as orderly as possible.

Slobs need not apply. If you can't work neatly, you won't work here.

One of the most important and overlooked area of any shop. A replica pit wall is just outside for pit-stop practice. Note the tape that marks where the car's right front tire should be.

A nice view to have from your workbench.

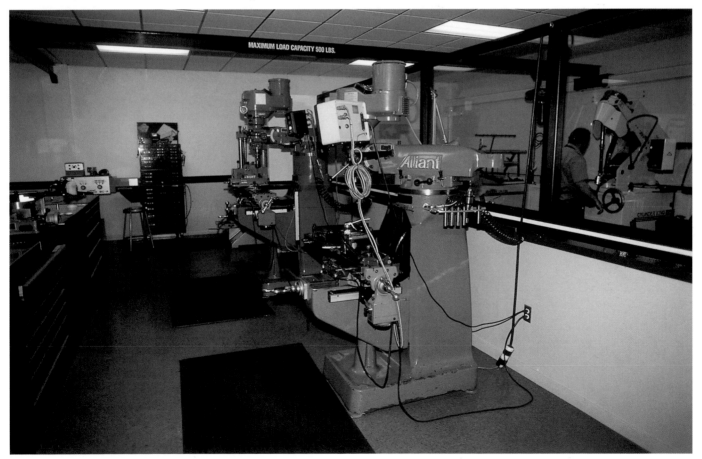

Conventional mills are still around for custom machining work.

Attention to detail extends to the most common of components. Everything is rebuilt and beefed up.

"Out back" allows for more storage.

The "Spin Tron." A recent development in engine testing. This machine has an electric motor that powers the test engine up to 9,000 rpm. Then, using a laser, crew members can make measurements on the valvetrain movement at high rpm.

THE HAULER

Everything the teams will need throughout qualifying, practice, and the race must be carried in their hauler. Haulers are as much a marvel as today's race cars. They must be able to hold two complete race cars (stored overhead), spare parts (including extra engines), tools (from wrenches to welding equipment), and all of the crew's personal equipment. Today's haulers can do all of this and still have enough room for a very comfortable lounge in the front of the trailer.

All the haulers park together at the track. It can be a tight fit, especially at the half-mile short tracks where the Busch Series and Winston Cup haulers all must be fit into the infield.

Cars are carried in the top of the trailer. Only the primary car is taken out at the track. Only if that is wrecked during practice or qualifying will the secondary car be unloaded.

Unloading Friday morning. The work area on the garage is pretty spartan. If you need it, you have to bring it on the truck.

Spare motors are carried in the lower inside cabinets.

At the front of the trailer, the driver and crew can relax in a small lounge. Even the lounges carry their load to the track.

A shock dyno is housed in the trailer. Shocks have become so important that there must be a test and rebuild facility on the truck.

A decent little "clean environment shop" is on the truck for delicate jobs.

Anything that the crew or the car
may need must be carried.
Pullout drawers house the
smaller components.

CHAPTER 4

When the team arrives at the track, the setup in the car is the "best guess," based on tests and past race experience. After a few practice laps the teams will begin trying to make it faster.

THE SETUP

Much of the race is over by the time the team arrives at the track, the large part of it being the search to find the perfect setup for that particular track. Preparing for a race begins long before arriving at the track. From practice sessions to dyno testing in the shop, teams test and retest setups. All the information gained during these tests will be used to decide on the way the car will be set up when the team arrives at the track. The more preparation for the race that can be done before leaving for the track, the better.

The setup is a combination of engine power, handling ability, braking ability, and aerodynamic qualities. Indeed, when cars and engines are built, the tracks on which they will run are the main influence on the design and building style. The goal of all of this preparation is to arrive at the track with the car ready to qualify and the race setup already decided.

Before leaving the shop, the engine setup is worked out on the dyno. Both the qualifying and race motors have been custom-tuned for the track being raced. This ensures that the car

Trying to find that perfect setup. The race in the garage is as important as the race on the track.

will produce power when the driver needs it the most. Engine power is an essential element in making a car go fast, but by far not the only element. In auto racing, three additional areas are important in producing a competitive car: good suspension setup, good brakes, and aerodynamic efficiency.

Engine power increases the speed of the car only as long as the suspension can efficiently transfer that power. Additional power does not help if it cannot be controlled. Smooth is fast, and an ill-handling car is not smooth.

Many complex physical forces are at work on a moving race car. Most of us have experienced some of these forces during our everyday driving, but not to the extremes encountered by the drivers on the tracks. A race car's handling ability is ultimately determined by the team's ability to adjust the suspension to counter these forces, and by the driver's ability to find the best line around the track to push the car to its limit, but not over it.

The forces affecting the handling of a race car vary with the position of the car on the track, whether the car is on a straight-away or

To refine the setup the teams will work on engine power...

. . . braking efficiency . . .

. . . suspension . . .

. . . and the car's aerodynamic efficiency.

Cars are usually built with a specific type of track in mind. A super-speedway car that is to run at Talladega will be very different from a short-track car that will run at Bristol. Below, cars at Talladega. . .

on a turn. In a turn, centrifugal force will try to sling the car outward; therefore, tracks are banked in varying degrees to counter this effect. As a rule, the higher the banking, the faster the cars can go. The 38 degree banking at Bristol allows incredible speeds on one of the smallest tracks. The qualifying speeds at Bristol last year were only about 50 miles per hour slower than qualifying speeds at Indianapolis. The Indianapolis track is 2.5 miles long, but it only has 4 degrees of banking in the turns, while Bristol is only a half-mile, but has 38 degrees of banking. The main difference in speed is due to the length of the straights at Indy, which skews the average lap speed to a higher number. (Incidentally, if you are a real NASCAR fan, do not grow old and die without seeing a race at Bristol. Pay what you must for a ticket. It's worth it.) To further illustrate this point, compare Bristol and Martinsville. The qualifying record at Bristol is around 125 mph (remember the 38 degree of banking). At Martinsville, another half-mile track, the qualifying record is only around 95 mph (with 12 degree banking). Centrifugal force is more

apparent to the race fan when the turns are not banked, but even with higher banking, the force is still there. It is simply being transferred elsewhere. Even though the turns are banked, teams must run stiffer springs on the right side to keep the car from bottoming out.

The suspension setup for a road-course car most closely resembles the suspension setup on a production car. These are the only Winston Cup cars set up to turn right as well as left at speed, just as production cars are. However, all cars raced on a circle track, be it a half-mile short track or a two-and-a-half-mile super speedway, are designed to turn well only to the left at speed. While turning, the right front tire carries the greatest amount of force. Next is the right rear, then the left front, with the left rear carrying the least amount of weight. Teams must match the spring rates in all four corners of the suspension to compensate for these differences in pressure. Indeed, it would be impossible turn a Winston Cup car around and drive it clockwise around the track at anywhere close to the speeds reached going counterclockwise.

. . . and cars at Bristol.

Cars run on tracks like Darlington may share some of the characteristics of a super-speedway car (a very aerodynamic body), and a short-track car (maximum brakes).

Some say that oversteer (top) happens when you don't see the wreck and understeer (bottom) happens when you do.

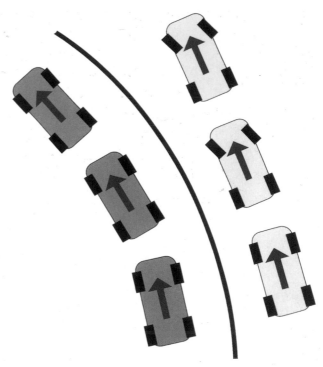

The red car illustrates a car oversteering, while the gray car illustrates a smooth, balanced turn.

The yellow car illustrates a car understeering, while the gray car illustrates a smooth, balanced turn.

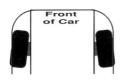

Toe-out condition: The front of the tire is pointed out, while the back of the tire is pointed in.

Negative Camber: The tires are tilted with the top in and the bottom out.

Negative Caster: The top of the ball-joint is set behind the centerline.

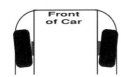

Toe-in condition: The front of the tire is pointed in while the back of the tire is pointed out.

Positive Camber: The tires are tilted with the top out and the bottom in.

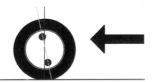

Positive Caster: The top of the ball-joint is set in front of the centerline.

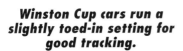

Winston Cup cars run a slightly toed-in setting for good tracking.

Camber is set in a slightly negative position to improve handling.

A slight positive caster setting allows for easier steering.

Aerodynamics are essential on the faster tracks. This body damage probably won't hurt much on a short track, but on a super speedway will turn you into an also-ran.

As with most things in life, a suspension change is always a compromise. The better-handling race car is the one set up closest to the edge of the adjustment compromises.

On road courses and shorter tracks, having power and a good suspension won't help if the brakes won't slow the car when entering the turn. If a driver has brake problems, he must either slow down using the engine and transmission (which places additional strain on the transmission and the rear end) or he must reduce his speed in the straight so that he won't be carrying as much speed into the turn. Either way, brake problems can quickly turn an otherwise competitive car into an also-ran.

Due to the variations in Winston Cup race tracks, the importance of each setup adjustment varies from track to track. On the longer tracks, aerodynamic efficiency becomes yet another area that must be considered. Some say it matters a great deal on shorter tracks also. Theoretically, the only time aerodynamics don't matter is when the car is sitting still. Slight changes in the bodywork on the car can have a dramatic effect on how efficiently the car cuts through the air.

The teams keep an eye on the weight distribution using portable scales. The amount of weight on each corner of the car may be adjusted using the lead weights carried in the chassis.

Each tire sits on an individual scale during weighing.

Wedge adjustments are adjustments made to the coil-spring pressure. A fixture is used to hold the top of the coil spring. By tightening or loosening this fixture, a person can increase or decrease the spring rate. This can dramatically influence the handling of the car.

A typical coil-spring suspension with jack bolts for wedge adjustments. The spring (purple) rides between the upper spring mount (orange) and the lower control arm on the bottom (yellow). The upper spring mount (orange) holds the top of the spring and is attached to the frame on top (blue) by the large jack bolt (black), which passes through a threaded fixture welded to the frame. When the jack bolt is tightened, the upper spring mount moves down, away from the frame, increasing the pressure on the spring and thus increasing the spring rate.

Rear spoiler angles are set before the race. The more the spoiler is laid down, the less drag it creates, but less down-force is also created, and the rear end of the car will be loose.

A race car's handling characteristics change during the race. The driver and the crew must work together during pit stops to make adjustments to the setup that can change the handling of a car. The following will give an idea of the general handling concerns that a team must focus on in order to be competitive during the race.

HANDLING TERMS AND SETUP ADJUSTMENTS

Just like all sports, racing has its own technical problems and the language to describe them.

The following section explains most of the handling problems and the common techniques used by the teams to refine the handling characteristics of their race car.

Oversteer

Also known as being loose, oversteer is a condition during which the car turns or steers too much. The rear of the car wants to swing out to the right.

Most of us have experienced oversteer in our everyday driving. If, while turning, you accelerated too much or hit a slick spot, the rear end of the car might have swung out, creating an oversteer situation. When this problem develops in a race car, the driver must compensate, usually by slowing down, both entering and through the turns, to avoid oversteer and having the car spin out.

Understeer

Also known as pushing, or as the car being tight, understeer is the tendency for the car to go straight when the front wheels are being turned (to continue to "push" forward). If you have ever hit a patch of ice or wet leaves as you were turning and braking at the same time, you experienced a pushing condition. The car

A lot of time is spent making sure the rear spoiler is the right size and is secured at the proper angle.

Proper air intake through the grill is essential. On short tracks this is not only for keeping the engine cool but also the brakes. If the grill openings become clogged, overheating may occur. At a super speedway, as much of the grill area as possible is taped off, because the brakes are only used for pitting.

continues to go forward even though you are turning the wheel. When this develops in a race car, the driver must slow down entering and going through the turns to avoid having the car push all the way into the wall. Obviously, the ride to the next pit stop is a long one when the car is pushing.

Alignment

Like a street car, a Winston Cup car has to be properly aligned to handle well. Street cars are aligned for proper "tracking" and for tire wear (50,000 miles or so). Race cars are aligned for proper tracking and maximum handling ability. All cars, street or race, have three basic alignment settings: toe, camber, and caster. Toe is the angle of the front of the tire and the rear of the tire relative to the centerline of the car. Camber is the angle of the top of the tire and the bottom of the tire relative to the vertical centerline of the tire. Caster is the angle between the ball-joints and the vertical centerline of the tire.

The alignment is set before the teams leave for the track. At the track it may be refined to improve tire wear or handling. Problems can occur during the race if the car gets "knocked out of alignment." Contact with the wall or other cars, running over a piece of debris, or running off the track can all result in the alignment being knocked out of its proper setting.

Aerodynamics

On longer intermediate tracks and super speedways, the aerodynamic flow (that is, the car's ability to cut through the air) becomes critical. Teams go to great levels to maximize a car's aerodynamic efficiency. They will use wind tunnels for testing and learning which small changes to the body improve the speed of cars being run at longer tracks. For instance, the

Stagger is based on the tire's outside diameter. Tires are measured with tape measures.

Tire pressure is the first line of adjustments. Changing the air pressure in one of the radial Goodyear tires changes the spring rate on that corner of the car.

hinges for the hood and deck lid may extend outside the body work on short-track and road-course cars, but they will be recessed on super-speedway cars. The total resistance given by these hinges is roughly equivalent to that of a sewing thimble glued to the hood of the car. But every little bit counts. If a car has body damage, its ability to cut through the air will be lessened, especially if the front fascia is damaged. Even minor dents can slow the car down on super speedways. On short tracks, aerodynamic flow is not as important and many battered race cars have made their way to victory lane, a few with no front body at all.

Wedge

"Wedge" is the name used to describe adjustments made to the coil springs to fine-tune the suspension setup. Wedge adjustments can be made on each corner of the suspension. Only wedge adjustments to the rear can be made without opening the hood, however.

The rear spring is mounted under the frame and the rear trailing arm. The upward pressure that the spring exerts on the frame is critical to a car's handling ability. Wedge adjustments are made by turning a bolt that runs through the frame rail and is attached to a fixture holding the top of the coil spring. By tightening the bolt, the spring is squeezed tighter, increasing the spring pressure or spring rate.

When wedge adjustments are necessary during pit stops, they are usually made on the rear springs. Tightening the left rear spring increases the spring rate and puts more pressure on the right front of the car. Likewise, lessening the spring rate on the left rear will take pressure off the right front tire.

This sounds more complicated than it is. If you take a small spring and squeeze it between your thumb and forefinger, the tighter you squeeze, the harder it becomes to continue to squeeze. That is, it takes much less strength to squeeze the first quarter-inch than the last quarter-inch. Wedge adjustments do the same thing to the car's coil springs. Now take a hardback book and balance it on a coffee cup so that the book is parallel to the table. If you barely lift on one corner, say the bottom left, then the top right corner will go down. Increasing the spring rate on the left rear of a race car will put more upward pressure on the

Tire temperature is checked often. The temperature is checked all over the tire to see how the setup is performing.

left rear of the frame and, just like with the book, a downward pressure will be exerted on the right front.

When adjusting wedge, the general rule of thumb is:

· Pressure taken off the front corrects a loose condition.

· Pressure taken off the rear corrects a tight condition.

If too much of an adjustment is made to correct understeer, then an oversteer problem may be created. Added to this is the different result attained by adjusting the left side spring as opposed to the right side spring. Crews must use great care in making even the smallest of wedge adjustments.

The Rear Spoiler

The rear spoiler dramatically influences how the race car handles. As air passes over the deck lid on the car it hits the spoiler; the higher the angle, the more resistance the air meets and the more downforce is created. A simple example of this principle can be experienced by holding your hand (flat, palm-down) out of a car

window at speed. By rotating your hand down at varying degrees, you can feel the air resistance change. The more you tilt, the more the wind pushes your hand down. The same principle holds true for the spoiler. There is a fine line between speed and control on longer tracks. The lower the angle of the spoiler, the less resistance, allowing the car to go faster in the straightaways. On the other hand, the car will not have as much downforce on the rear and is much more likely to be loose and difficult to control in the turns. Too much spoiler and the car will have plenty of down-force for the turns but will suffer on the straights.

Grill Openings

A certain amount of air must pass through the front grill to cool the engine. This open grill area creates drag. The bigger the opening, the greater the drag and the lower the speed. Likewise, the smaller the opening, the less the drag and the greater the speed. Teams may reduce the size of the openings by taping over some of the grill opening with duct tape. Taping over the grill can be used as an adjustment only when it will not critically affect

Probably the most important factor in determining the best setup is good driver-crew chief communication. Just ask Jeff Gordon and Ray Evernham.

engine cooling. It is often used in qualifying and toward the end of the race if circumstances permit pit stops.

Fender Support Rods

Winston Cup cars have support rods that keep the fenders rigid. These rods have adjustable sleeves that can be lengthened or shortened. This is another aerodynamic adjustment that can affect speed and handling by changing the position of the edge of the fender in relation to the edge of the tire. A change in airflow around the fender wells and tires can have a substantial influence on speed at super speedways. This adjustment is usually refined during wind tunnel testing and practice, and is seldom, if ever, changed during the race.

Stagger

Stagger is an adjustment made by using different-sized tires on the car at the same time. Teams put tires on the outside of the car that have a slightly larger diameter than the tires on the inside of the car. This allows the car to turn more efficiently on circular tracks when the car makes only left turns. This principle can be seen by placing a light bulb next to a rolling pin on a flat surface and rolling both of them. The rolling pin rolls straight while the light bulb turns in a circle because of the difference in stagger between the inside and outside diameters.

Tire Pressure

Adjusting tire pressure is a good example of how the smallest of changes can make a dramatic difference in a car's handling. In a street car, a couple pounds of variation in tire pressure will not affect performance and will not be noticeable to the driver. In a race car, however, the handling characteristics can be drastically changed by varying the tire pressure among the four tires. A few pounds more or less in a particular tire can fine-tune the handling of a race car. The more pressure in a tire, the stiffer the sidewall of a tire becomes. As with springs and shocks, this sidewall stiffness can be controlled and used to fine-tune the setup.

Changes in the temperature of the tire also affect tire pressure. For every 10 degrees of increased tire temperature, the air pressure in the tire will increase 1 lb. This means that after a run, if a tire is 70 degrees hotter than when the run started, there will be 7 more lb of air pressure in the tire. Tire temperatures are monitored closely by the crews. Temperatures vary from track to track. Longer tracks with extended straightaways and gradual turns do not heat up tires nearly as much as the flatter, short tracks where the car is turning more, and the scrubbing action between the tire and the track is more severe. When setting up the suspension, crews try to achieve diagonal balance between the tires. Diagonal balance is the relationship between the left rear and the right front, and the right rear and the left front. If, at the end of a run, the right front tire temperature is 200 degrees and the left rear is 190 degrees, the car is said to have 10 degrees of push. Likewise, if the right front is 190 and the left rear 200, the car is 10 degrees loose. The optimal setup balances the tire temperature between these diagonal corners.

Possibly the most important factor in a team's success is the ability of a driver and the crew to discuss the car's performance. A winning driver must have a competitive car, and the setup is the greatest determining factor in having one. Good communication is very important in refining the setup. The driver must be able to tell the crew exactly what the car is doing, and then the crew and driver must evaluate the situation and decide on correcting adjustments. If the driver and the crew cannot communicate accurately when "dialing in," that is, finding the optimum settings for the car, hitting a good setup will be difficult.

The trucks roll in early Friday. The garage area usually opens around six a.m.

AT THE TRACK

TO THE TRACK: RACE WEEKEND

By Thursday night, the team haulers are already in town. The track usually opens around six for the trucks to enter the garage area. Once the team and rig arrive, the work really begins: The temporary garage must be set up, the car unloaded, and everything made ready for qualifying and race practice. Then the garage area really becomes a beehive of activity

right up until the race begins. Between practice runs on the track, the car is rolled back to the garage area for adjustment Although the work area is limited (each team has one stall), the work done is pretty much limitless. Be it major bodywork or swapping motors or rear ends, the professionalism of the crew shows here, perhaps, more than anywhere else. Changing

The first order of business is to unload the truck. Everything necessary for the race weekend is carried in the rig.

major components in just a few minutes is routine. With limited time for both qualifying practice and race practice, less time spent in the garage means more time spent on the track, and the better chance of dialing in the winning setup.

QUALIFYING

On Friday, the first order of business is getting the car ready for qualifying. Most teams arrive at the track with a dedicated qualifying engine that is set up a little more on the edge than the race engines. After all, they only have to last a

few laps, whereas the race engine must last 500 miles. The car arrives at the track with the qualifying engine in it, ready to go. During morning practice, teams try to dial in the suspension setup.

The first setup tried will most likely be based on previous experience at that particular track or on a recent test session. Teams may start with the same setup they ran well with at a previous race under basically the same track and weather conditions. As qualifying practice starts, lap times are tracked and the driver's observations about how the car is behaving are discussed. Qualifying practice usually consists

It's amazing how much is brought to the track. Here, a pair of motors waits to come down the loft. Teams will come to the track with the qualifying motor in the car. A race motor and a few spares will also be needed.

The car and tools are moved to the garage area. This will be the center of activity for the team until race day.

At short tracks like Bristol there is no garage. Most of the work is done outside.

of two lap runs, and then back to the garage for adjustments. Teams may change tire combinations, tire pressure, spring rates, shock settings, wedge adjustments, sway bar combinations, spoiler angles, or even rear-end gear ratios.

A makeshift shop may be set up behind the hauler. The lift at the back of the hauler gives some welcome shade.

At super speedways, small body details such as the relationship of the fender to the edge of the tire and airflow around the grill are refined. Crews are always looking for slight aerodynamic improvements that could well mean a thousandth of a second during qualifying.

In years past, many "qualifying only" parts were put on the cars. For instance, until recently, a different, dedicated qualifying radiator was used. Now the rules require that a car must race with the radiator that it had when it qualified, eliminating "qualifying radiators," which could not properly cool the engine for 500 miles. Once the team feels that the car is running competitively enough to qualify, practicing stops and the wait for qualifying begins.

Usually, a race has a field of around 42 race cars. Qualifying order is determined by a draw before qualifying begins. Cars qualify one at a time. Normally, qualifying consists of a two-lap run, with the fastest of the two laps being the

It can be a tight fit in the garage area. All day Friday and Saturday, it is a beehive of activity. On Friday teams work on the qualifying setup. If they make the top 25 in qualifying, they will begin working on the race setup. Those who don't qualify on Friday will either have to stand on their time, try to qualify again on Saturday, or take a provisional starting place.

Qualifying practice is first on Friday's track session. Practice consists of running a couple of laps and then adjusting the car. The qualifying setup must only be fast for two laps. The cars form a steady line back and forth from the track to the garage and back to the track.

qualifying time. All qualifying runs start from a standstill and from the same point on pit road. The first lap time starts when the car has circled the track and crossed the start/finish line, already up to speed. If a car experiences a problem on the second qualifying lap, the first lap time may still be used. Usually only the first 25 positions are decided on the first day of qualifying. Positions 26–42 are decided on the second day of qualifying. Race cars that did not qualify for positions 1–25 may attempt to qualify again. On the second day of qualifying, the fastest time is assigned the 21st starting position and so on until all positions in the field are taken.

If a car does not qualify for the race in either session, it may still be able to race. "Provisional" starting positions are available, but they are always at the end of the field. The recipients of these positions are decided by the points accumulated by the car owner. The only other provisional qualifying positions are for past champions. Drivers who have won the Winston

Cup Championship have a lifetime ticket for provisional starting positions.

Qualifying for the Daytona 500 is different from any other race. Initial qualifying is just as described above; however, only the front row (starting positions 1 and 2) is decided. The rest

The team has to make time for meals, and the food is usually good. Much of it is cooked in the garage area.

Safety comes first in Winston Cup racing. Cars are always placed securely on jack stands before anyone crawls under them.

of the qualifying speeds are used to determine the starting order of two 125-mile qualifying races. The finishing orders of the 125-mile races determine positions 3–38. The remaining fastest qualifiers from initial qualifying and provisional starters complete the field.

During qualifying and practice, crew chiefs and crew members watch the competition from viewing stands on top of the haulers.

The activity on Friday and Saturday is ruled by the stopwatch. The routine is to run laps, check the lap time, make an adjustment, and check the time again. The search for more speed never stops.

PRACTICE

Once qualifying is completed, teams shift gears and begin to set up the car for the race. The qualifying engine is taken out of the car and replaced with the race engine. After the motor is swapped, teams change from their qualifying setup to the race setup. The race suspension must be fast and also comfortable for the driver

During qualifying only one car at a time is on the track. It's the driver against the stopwatch.

Race practice runs are longer. Drivers stay out on long runs to see how the car handles as the tires wear and the fuel load lightens. Drivers will mix it up during practice to see how their car handles in traffic.

for 500 miles. While qualifying practice runs are one or two laps long, the race practice runs are longer. A qualifying setup must be as fast as possible, and that speed must be reached as quickly as possible. Since a qualifying run is only two laps long, a setup that is fast after eight laps does not help much. A race setup, on the other hand, must be fast over long runs. A setup that is fast for two laps and then fades may qualify well, but does not do much for the team in the actual race. Over long runs during the race, the car changes. For example, tires progressively lose their grip the longer they are run. As the fuel is used, each gallon burned means around 6 lb of weight out of the fuel cell. Twenty gallons means around 120 lb, which can make quite a difference in the handling. Once all of the setup changes have been made final, the cars go back out and practice, recording lap speeds and adjusting the engine and suspension.

The most critical practice session comes after the Saturday main event. For one hour, Winston Cup cars are allowed to practice, doing their final tuning and setup preparation.

Only part of the field is allowed on the track during practice. It's first come, first served. Cars will line up and be allowed to go on the track as others come off.

Throughout the race weekend, fuel is supplied by Unocal and dispensed from pumps in the garage area. During practice and qualifying, the cars are gassed at the pump.

Known as Happy Hour, this is the last time cars are allowed to practice before the Sunday race. Any car that is wrecked beyond repair during practice may be replaced with a backup car, but the car forfeits its starting position and must start the race at the rear of the field.

FUEL

Fuel for practice, qualifying, and the race is currently supplied by Unocal. The high 104 octane allows teams to run the high-compression engines seen in today's Winston Cup cars. Unocal operates a pump station throughout the race weekend. During practice, the cars are pushed to the pump, and the gas is pumped directly into the car. Throughout the race, though, the fuel cans used to fill the car during pit stops are filled at the pump station and the crews use small carts to pull the cans back to the pit.

TIRES

Goodyear sets up shop in the garage area and is available to sell, mount, and balance tires for the teams. The rubber compound used in the tires varies from track to track. Throughout the event, a close eye is kept on tire pressures and

Tires are all Goodyear Racing Eagles.

There are complete facilities for mounting and balancing in the garage area.

tire wear. Because tire temperature has such an effect on tire pressure and tire wear, tire temperatures are measured after each run and are taken from different spots on the tire to check the relationship of the inside to the outside of the tires.

Teams will rack up quite a tire bill over the weekend—a minimum of around 10 sets of tires at over $1,000 a set.

Before qualifying and racing, the cars must pass through the room of doom. Throughout the weekend NASCAR officials check many points of the car to make sure it is within the rules. If a car fails it will have to be fixed, and the inspection process will begin again.

SECTION 5.2 INSPECTION

All competing cars are inspected before each race and may be inspected at any time during and after the race. Due to the fact that all race cars will be somewhat different, inspection procedures take place not only to catch premeditated cheating but also to ensure maximum competitiveness. Race cars are built by different people, in different places, at different times, with parts from different suppliers, all using the same rules—which can be interpreted in a variety of ways. Indeed, just as teams must constantly look for an edge in their engine and chassis, they must constantly look for edges in the rule book, finding different ways to go faster while staying within NASCAR's rule specifications. In building the cars, teams interpret the rules in search of slight advantages that might provide the edge on the track. With the number of cars competing and the number of parts on a Winston Cup car, inspecting for violations is a difficult job for the officials. It is impossible for the rule makers to think of everything, but the teams usually will. Inspection procedures ensure that the "spirit" of the rules is observed, again keeping the playing field as level as possible.

The inspection zone is set up in the garage area.

The body profile is checked all over. With aerodynamics playing such a major role, many different locations are checked.

The car's weight is checked on NASCAR's scales.

At the track, the inspection area is used by all the teams before and during practice runs to ensure that changes made in the setup don't take the car out of tolerance. These "self-inspections" ensure that the setup being tested is legal and prevents any embarrassing moments during formal inspections. Cars may be sealed or impounded, and fines levied if rule violations are found.

Roof height is measured with a simple go, no-go gauge. A green reading means the car passes. Red means it's too low. The exact point at which the roof is measured is located by the NASCAR official.

The carburetor and air cleaner are checked. How the car draws air is very important, especially at restricter plate tracks.

Pressure tests may be done to the intake manifold at restricter plate tracks to make sure that no air is being "accidentally" pulled through the manifold.

The air dam and body height is checked. If the block does not slide under the car, it's too low.

Once the car has cleared inspection, it can wear the NASCAR sticker.

SECTION 5.3 · RACE DAY

Sunday morning finds many teams still at work. It is not uncommon to find many of the cars in varying states of repair. As the teams finish this preparation, the cars are pushed to their position on the starting grid. The cars, or at least the windshields, are covered to keep the interiors cool. A cart with a generator accompanies each car. The generator provides power for heaters that are used to keep up the oil temperature. Once the cars are on the starting grid, they will not be cranked until the race begins.

Early Sunday morning the teams begin to set up the pit stall. The pit carts are remarkable. Tools, spare parts, television. Just about anything the team needs will go to the pit in the carts.

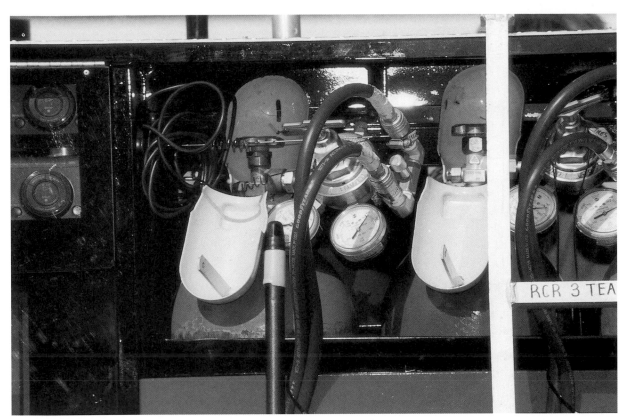

Air pressure for pit stops is supplied from tanks in the pit cart.

Air guns are made ready and air lines neatly coiled.

Water is carried to the pits in a rollable tank. If the car overheats and water has to be put in the radiator, this is where it comes from.

Tires are laid out in sets for the many pit stops.

The lug nut process begins. In order to accomplish those fast pit stops the teams must first glue the lug nuts to the wheels. First the wheel is cleaned, especially around the bolt holes.

Glue is applied to the edge of the lug nuts and the lug nut is placed on the wheel.

Weights are set on the lug nuts to make sure they are seated well while the glue dries.

The finished product. Now the tire changer can place the wheel on the studs, pick up his wrench, and tighten away.

Everything that will be needed for routine and not so routine pit stops must be brought. In case of body damage, a couple of big hammers may be a necessity. The big ugly club to the right in this photo can be used to roll out crimped fenders.

Pit Stall

Sunday morning, teams begin to set up the pit stall. First, the cart containing tools, parts, and the air tanks for the air wrenches is pushed to the pit stall. In recent years, many carts have been equipped with a video setup to tape pit stops (the camera is extended over the pit area on a lightweight boom), and even small satellite dishes enabling teams to monitor the television broadcast of the race.

The teams must be as ready as possible for those "nonroutine" pit stops. Minor body, suspension, and engine problems can be fixed in the pits, but only if the crew thought ahead and had the parts and tools ready when the problem occurred. A trip back to the hauler to get something may cost the team lots of track position.

Pit equipment has become as sophisticated as the cars. The equipment used in making pit stops can be as important as equipment on the car. The variety of tools used in the pits continues to grow. More than one race has been lost when a jack or air wrench malfunctioned.

Starting the Race

On Sunday morning the team does its final preparation to the car. Once the car is finished, it is inspected and pushed to the starting grid.

At the beginning of the race, the pace car leads the field through a couple of laps. During these "pace laps," cars on the starting grid can resume their place if they drop out of position. After one or two pace laps a driver can duck into the pits, top off the fuel supply, and resume position before the race starts. This may give a car one more lap under green flag racing. That might come in handy later.

If a car drops out completely on the first lap, its finishing position is determined by its

Having a few sheets of duct tape ready can save time. Teams make these patches before the race, stick them to the side of the tool cart and hope they will not need them.

As some crew members are setting up the pits, others are still preparing the car. Everything on the car is checked before the car goes to inspection. Once a car clears inspection, it will go to the starting grid.

starting position in relation to the starting position of the other cars that dropped out on the first lap. In order for the initial driver of a car to receive points, that driver must start the race. If the initial driver does not start the race, the relief driver accumulates the points and winnings. This is why an injured driver may start the race and quickly switch to a backup driver.

Once past inspection the teams push the cars to the starting grid.

Once the cars are on the starting grid they are ready to go. Generators are used to keep the oil warm. Electric strip heaters are attached to the oil reservoir tank. The power is plugged in at the back of the car.

The cars are covered and await the start of the race.

PIT STOPS

A typical four-tire, full-tank-of-gas, clean-the-windshield-and-the-front-grill pit stop. All accomplished, on average, in about 18 or 19 seconds. The great pit stop crews get it done in 17 seconds or less.

With the introduction of speed limits on pit road, in recent years, the distance lost on the track while pitting has become much greater. Teams must carefully choose when to pit in order to minimize the lost track position. Caution flags provide the best time for pitting; however, inevitably teams will be forced to pit during green flag racing, or while the racing remains at full speed. For every second a cars sits in the pits, it loses distance on the track relative to the race speed.

Over the last few years, pit stops and pit strategy have probably been as responsible for victories as any other factor. Three things can happen during a pit stop: A car can gain position, lose position, or stay in the same position.

Drivers who win races seem to be the ones who do a lot of "passing in the pits." Beating competitors in the pits means less work on the track. It may take 20 laps on the track to pass another car. A crew can pass that same car in the pits while the driver drinks a glass of water.

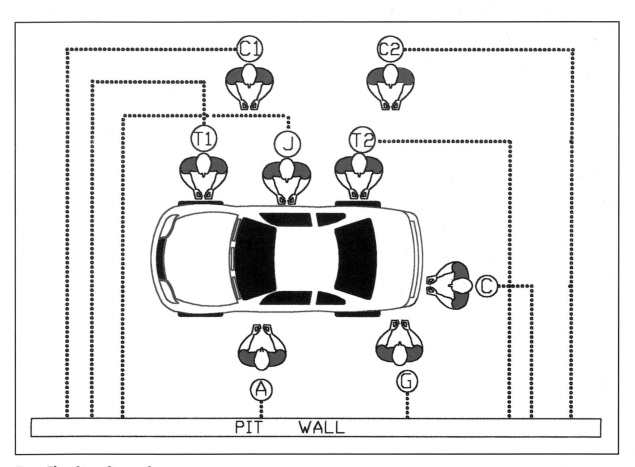

Four Tire Stop Stage One

J (Jack Man): Runs around the front of car, places the jack under the jack point and jacks up the right side (current jacks allow the car to be lifted with only one stroke of the jack).

T1 (Front Tire Changer): Runs around the front of the car with an air gun and loosens the wheel (5 lug nuts) on the right front, removes the tire wheel assembly, places the new tire onto the car and tightens the lug nuts.

C1 (Front Tire Carrier): Carries the new right tire around the front of car, helps the tire changer place the wheel on the car and then removes the old right front tire.

T2 (Rear Tire Changer): Runs around the rear of the car with an air gun and loosens the wheel on the right rear, removes the tire wheel assembly, places the new tire onto the car and tightens the lug nuts.

C2 (Rear Tire Carrier): Carries new right rear tire around the rear of car, helps the tire changer place the wheel on the car and then removes the old right rear tire.

G (Gas Man): Places refill tank spout into the fitting at the left rear of the car and begins to fill the car's fuel tank.

C (Catchcan Man): Places the overflow container in overflow tube located on the left side of the decklid and catches any fuel that overflows preventing it from spilling onto the pit road.

A (Assistant): It may be permitted to have an extra man over the wall to clean the windshield.

If two cars are equally matched, they may be able to stay with each other on the track but not be able to pass each other. The pits may be the only place where one can gain an advantage over the other. This is why winning drivers typically compliment their crew when climbing out of the car in victory lane.

An extra second with the car on the jack can mean two or three cars to pass on the track. Even if these cars can be overtaken easily, the driver will use up a little more of his tires each time he passes one of them. This means his car will fade quicker than other cars that don't have to pass as much.

Although performing the required work quickly and correctly is essential to a good pit stop, it is only a part. Perhaps just as important as the work, if not more so, is the pit stop strategy. First, the crew chief must communicate with the driver via radio and develop an understanding of how the car is handling. By using only the driver's descriptions, the spotter's

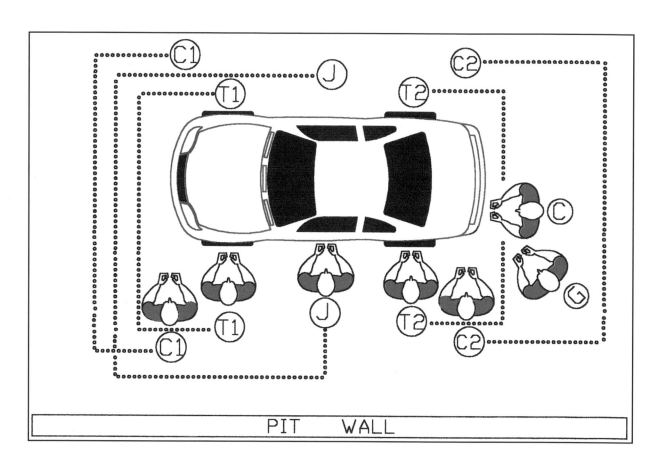

Four Tire Stop Stage Two
J: Runs back around the front of the car, places the jack under the jack point and jacks up the left side. When the left side tires are on, the jack man drops the car and the driver takes off.

T1: Runs back around the front of car with air gun and loosens the wheel on the left front, removes the tire wheel assembly, places the new tire onto the car and tightens the lug nuts.

C1: Gets new left front tire, carries it to the tire changer, helps tire changer place the wheel on the car and then removes the old left front tire.

T2: Runs back around the rear of car with air gun and loosens the wheel on the left rear, removes the tire wheel assembly, places the new tire onto the car and tightens the lug nuts.

C2: Gets new left rear tire, carries it to tire changer, helps tire changer place the wheel on the car and then removes the old left rear tire.

G: Empties first can of fuel into car, hands it off and receives second can of fuel and fills.

C: Continues to catch overflow and assists gas man as necessary.

observations, and the lap speeds, the crew chief makes a decision as to how the setup will be adjusted. Once the decision is made as to what will be adjusted, the crews must decide how much to adjust it. If a "loose" car is overadjusted, it may become tight, slowing the car even more. On a race afternoon, a crew chief's chain of thought may be something like this:

"The car's a little loose with new tires but after about 20 laps, as the fuel load lightens, it tightens up the car and lap times pick up. But it's killing the team on restarts because the car falls back and has to repass the same cars that passed us during those first 20 laps. Is it better to do nothing, and keep relatively the same track position, or make an adjustment to quicken the car on those first twenty laps and risk ruining the good handling characteristics we'll experience later in the run?"

This simple scenario is one of a myriad of situations that a crew chief may encounter during the race. Often, the crew chief's problems

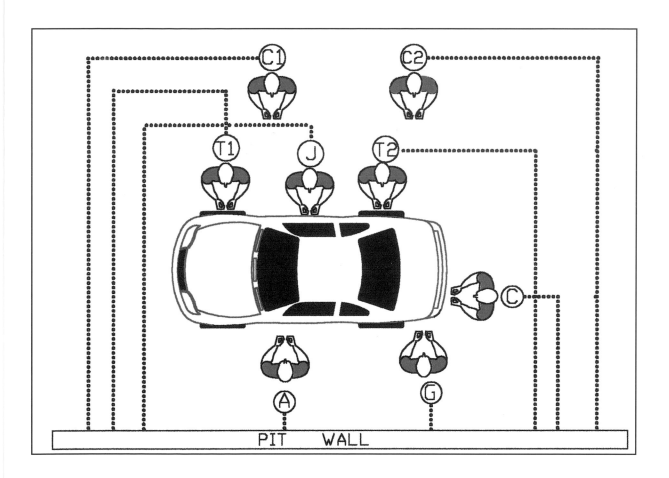

Two Tire Stop Stage One
J: Runs around the front of car, places the jack under the jack point and jacks up the right side.
T1: Runs around the front of the car with an air gun and loosens the wheel on the right front, removes the tire wheel assembly, places the new tire onto the car and tightens the lug nuts.
C1: Carries new right front tire around the front of car, helps the tire changer place the wheel on the car and then removes the old right front tire.
T2: Runs around the rear of the car with an air gun and loosens the wheel on the right rear, removes the tire wheel assembly, places the new tire onto the car and tightens the lug nuts.
C2: Carries new right rear tire around the rear of car, helps the tire changer place the wheel on the car and then removes the old right rear tire.
G: Places refill tank spout into the fitting at the left rear of the car and begins to fill the car's fuel tank.
C: Places the overflow container in overflow tube located on the left side of the decklid and catches any fuel that overflows preventing it from spilling onto the pit road.
A: It may be permitted to have an extra man over the wall to clean the windshield.

A blown motor will end a day quickly. Incredibly, this happens seldomly, given all the strain put on the engine!

soft race tires, often clog the grill. If they get past the grill, they can clog the radiator, thereby reducing its ability to cool the engine. A car encountering debris finds that the debris can remain pressed against the grill and cut off the airflow to the radiator and oil cooler.

If the overheating involves an internal engine problem, chances are the team cannot correct it on the spot. All that can be done is to make sure that as much coolant as possible is kept in the cooling system. If the overheating is caused by grill obstructions, the crew can try to clean out the grill during pit stops. If the grill or radiator has become clogged with tire rubber, however, the degree to which it can be cleaned is limited.

A blown tire can put a driver into the wall. If he is lucky, he can get to the pits and change it without wrecking the car.

Lost Cylinder

When a car is said to have "lost a cylinder," the engine has experienced some type of internal failure, causing it to quit making power in one of its eight cylinders. While such a failure may not be bad enough to completely stop an engine, it is a very serious problem. Obviously the engine has lost at least one-eighth of its ability to build power, and it is running out of balance, far out of its design range. These problems, as well as the possibility of a broken component interfering with another component, can cause further engine damage, often resulting in a lost cylinder advancing to total engine failure.

A lost cylinder is usually the result of a valvetrain problem. Either a rocker arm, valve spring, or valve has broken or otherwise stopped functioning. When a car has lost a cylinder, there is very little a team may do to correct the problem. The driver usually keeps the car on the track, nursing it around and accumulating as many laps as possible for championship points.

Ignition

The electronic ignition system used in Winston Cup racing provides and controls the spark that fires the engine. If this system fails, the engine will run poorly or quit altogether. Winston Cup cars carry two ignition modules, both mounted inside the car, next to the driver.

Some incidents end with no more than a car pointed in the wrong direction.

Others end with two cars trying to occupy the same space, and that's where the problems occur.

Damage is inevitable. Teams will try to repair cars to get as many points as possible.

If the first fails, the driver can switch to the backup. If the second unit fails, the team must take a lengthy pit stop to install a new unit.

Pre-detonation

Pre-detonation is the most common cause of piston failure. The typical modern production engine has a compression ratio of 8.5 to 1. This ratio is calculated by dividing the volume of the cylinder at the bottom of the stroke (the top of the piston at the bottom of the cylinder) by the volume of the cylinder at the top of the stroke (the top of the piston at the top of the cylinder).

Winston Cup cars run compression ratios of around 12 to 1. In a properly functioning engine, the mixture of air and fuel in the cylinder is ignited or detonated (near the top of the stroke) by the spark plug. Pre-detonation takes place when the fuel/air mixture is ignited too soon by the pressure of compression, before the piston is at the point of the stroke where ignition of the fuel/air mixture should take place. The piston then continues upward, further compressing the exploding fuel air/mixture and causing further detonations. Then the spark plug fires, re-detonating the whole mess. This series of detonations builds up more heat than a proper, one-time firing at the top of the stroke. As this heat builds, it can burn a hole all the way through the top of the piston, causing total engine failure.

Engine Failure

Many things can go wrong with an engine, causing it to quit or blow, but in reality, few engines in Winston Cup racing do. With Winston Cup engines turning plus or minus 9,000 rpm for 500 miles, it is surprising that more engines don't experience catastrophic failure. A list of all of the causes of engine failure would be quite a publication in itself. Most engine failures can be classified into four types: random failure, design-growth failure, support-system failure, or driver error.

Random engine failure is caused either by a bad part, a part that was not properly installed, or a combination of the two. Improper heat treating; internal, nonvisible manufacturing flaws; or parts that have been overstressed can fail in an instant with no warning. If, during installation, a part is damaged, contaminated, or bolted or torqued too tight (or not tight enough), failure can be imminent.

Sometimes the car is a total write-off. The good news is that drivers usually walk away.

Periodic design-growth failures can affect more than one team during a season. As engine speeds increase, there is a period of time during which more stress is put on a particular component. Teams must then work with suppliers to redesign the part to withstand the new pressures being applied. For instance, there were a number of engine failures for a while due to the failure of valve springs. Engine speeds were too fast for the valve springs to consistently open and close without severely stressing their limits. Suppliers had to find new designs that could consistently withstand the new stresses. The problem was eventually solved, but in the process, the engine was able to turn faster, and inevitably the next

This is why the roll bar rules are so tight. A super-speedway accident can be vicious. Bill Elliott was able to race the next week after this horrible wreck.

weakest link in the engine will surface. Perhaps in this case it will be the push rods. When the next problem surfaces, the whole process will begin again. The solution to one problem moves the teams closer to the next series of periodic design-growth failures.

Support-system failure is an engine failure brought on by a support system's loss of efficiency or failure. For example, if the radiator becomes clogged, spectators may not notice it, but they will notice when the loss of cooling efficiency causes a cylinder head to crack. This failure was not caused by the cylinder head itself or the man who installed it; rather, it happened because the engine was put into a position of performing beyond its design criteria.

Drivers can also "blow" an engine. A missed shift can over-rev an engine, causing failure. Or, if a driver pulls in behind another car at 190 miles per hour, the reduced air resistance encountered in drafting can cause a slight increase in the rpm of the engine. If the motor is already red-lined, this may be all it takes to blow it.

Body Damage

Body damage impacts the performance of the car differently depending on where the damage occurs and on what type of track the race is being run. Slight dents along the side of the car will not have much of an impact on short tracks and road courses, but they may ruin a car's competitiveness on longer tracks.

Some places on the car are more vulnerable than others. Damage to the left front of the car can be fatal, whereas the same damage to the right front of the car would not stop it from racing. The oil cooler is mounted just behind the sheet metal in the left front corner. If the cooler is damaged, the engine will not last. If the cooler is punctured or supply lines are ripped loose, a patch of oil will drop on the track for all the other drivers to enjoy. Likewise, damage to the left rear can damage the fuel inlet, hindering refueling during pit stops. If the car is hit broadside against a wheel, the car may be knocked out of alignment.

All the driver can do is wait. Here, Ken Schrader waits to see if he will be able to make a few more laps before the race ends. If he does, he will finish ahead of all drivers in the wreck that could not return to the action. At this point the race was under the red flag, and the crew cannot work on the car.

CHAPTER 6

RULES AND REFERENCE

The action at the track is monitored closely by NASCAR officials. Teams are provided with the NASCAR rule book and are required to live by it. The following text describes some of the rules and regulations that the teams must follow to race legally.

THE FLAGS
Green Flag

Displayed to Start or Restart the race. When the race is started, the cars must maintain their positions until the start/finish line is crossed. On restarts the racing begins as soon as the flag is displayed.

Yellow Flag

Displayed immediately after a cause for Caution. Cars may "race back" to the flag, as the order they finish the lap during which the flag was displayed will determine the restart order. Cars line up single file on the track behind the pace car until time to restart.

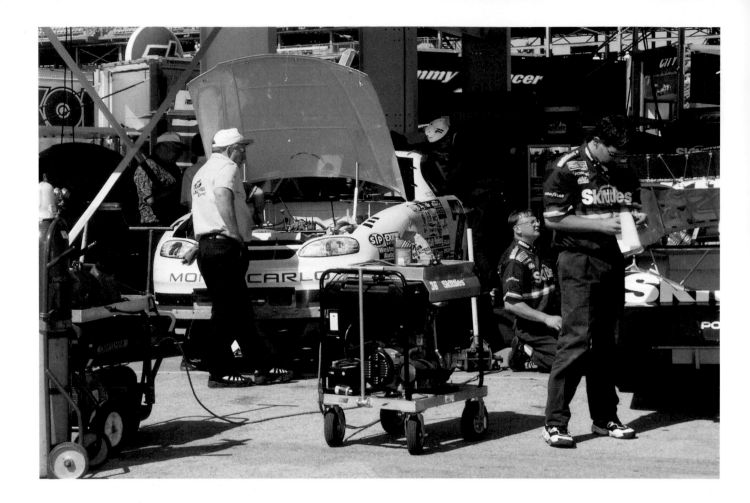

Black Flag

Displayed to order a particular car to the pits immediately, usually because the car may not be safe or because of driver actions. If ignored, the black flag with a white cross is displayed.

Black Flag with White Cross

Displayed to indicate a car has ceased to be scored for ignoring the black flag.

Red Flag

Displayed to stop the race when conditions make it unsafe to race. Cars are lined up in a designated area, and no work may be done to them until the race is restarted.

Passing Flag

Displayed to indicate a passing situation. Cars on the track about to be passed by faster cars are shown this flag to let them know what is happening. This flag is usually displayed to cars about to be overtaken by the race leaders.

White Flag

Displayed to indicate that the race leader has started the last lap of the race. If the yellow and white flags are both displayed, the race will end under caution.

Checkered Flag

Displayed at the completion of the race. All cars on the track receive the checkered flag on the last lap, their final positions all being relative to the race winner.

LICENSES

Drivers, car owners, and crew members must have a current NASCAR license in order to take part in Winston Cup Series events. The license recognizes the person as a participant only in a specific capacity. Licenses are obtained through the NASCAR general headquarters. To procure a license, a person must be at least 16 years of age, must meet the physical fitness requirements set by NASCAR, and, in the case of drivers, may have to pass a driving test. A car owner must also obtain a license from NASCAR for a car to be eligible to compete. It is during this licensing process that cars are given their numbers. Drivers aren't issued numbers, nor do they own them. The car number is issued to and owned by the car owner.

ENTRY PROCEDURE

Each race requires filling out an entry form before competing. The entry form lists, among other things, the date, total purse, payoff per finishing position, and bonus awards (television awards, qualifying awards, and manufacturers' prize money). The entry form also lists the eligibility requirements, qualifying rules, and any other special conditions that exist at a particular track. The names of the drivers and car owners, the license number and type of car, the car sponsor, and appropriate signatures are required. There are two sections to the entry application. One is sent to the race promoter, the other to NASCAR.

RESPONSIBILITY

The crew chief is the sole spokesman for the car owner and driver, and during the event he must assume responsibility for the actions of the driver and the crew. If problems arise, the crew chief is subject to disciplinary action.

Drivers are responsible for being on time for all required events. Should they be late or miss a drivers' meeting, they can be sent to the rear of the starting line, or not be allowed to race at all. If the driver on a team needs to be changed, officials must be given advance notice.

STARTING ORDER DETERMINATION

Drivers can attempt to qualify only one car. The qualifying time is accredited to the car, not the driver. In the event the approved driver is changed, the car's qualifying position is not changed. If a car is wrecked beyond repair during practice after it has qualified, a backup car may be used. The backup car brought to the track, however, cannot be unloaded from the truck unless approved. Backup cars start at the rear of the field, since they did not qualify. If qualifying is rained out, the order is determined by the current Winston Cup point standings.

The fastest qualifier, or pole car, is usually given the choice of the inside or outside position on the first row, and is used as the control car on starts. The fastest qualifier must lead the first lap of the race. Any car passing the pole car before it crosses the start/finish line will be penalized; usually a "stop and go" penalty is assessed.

INSPECTIONS

All competing cars are inspected before each race and may be inspected at any time during and after the race. Since all race cars will be somewhat different, inspection procedures take place not only to catch premeditated cheating but also to ensure maximum competitiveness. Race cars are built by different people, in different places, at different times, with parts from different suppliers, all using the same rules.

These rules can be interpreted in a variety of ways. Indeed, just as teams must constantly look for an edge in their engine and chassis, they must constantly look for edges in the rule book, finding different ways to go faster while staying within NASCAR's rule specifications. While building the cars, teams interpret the rules in search of slight advantages that might provide the edge on the track. With the number of cars competing and the number of parts on a Winston Cup car, inspecting for violations is a difficult job for the officials.

It is impossible for the rule makers to think of everything, but the teams usually will. Inspection procedures ensure that the "spirit" of the rules is observed, again keeping the playing field as level as possible.

At the track, the inspection area is used by all the teams before and during practice runs to ensure that changes made in the setup don't take the car out of tolerance. These "self-inspections" ensure that the setup being tested is legal and prevents any embarrassing moments during formal inspections. Cars may be sealed or impounded, and fines levied if rule violations are found.

If the track becomes unfit for racing, the race must be stopped. This can be a result of weather, a bad accident, or damage to the track that creates unsafe conditions for the drivers and fans. Cars are stopped and lined up in the order in which they were running after the completion of the last lap. If a race is stopped, cars cannot be worked on. If a car is already in the pits or garage area being worked on, all work must stop until the race is resumed.

Should a race event be stopped, it can be restarted as long as time permits. Should the race be stopped and racing can not be resumed, the event will be rescheduled for a later date. If half or more of the race has been completed when stopped, and racing cannot be resumed, then the race will be declared official and the running order at the time of the race stoppage will be the final finishing order. This is why it is so critical to be at the front of the pack when rain is threatening.

POINTS DETERMINATION

The Winston Cup Championship is determined by the number of points accumulated by each driver during the season. Each race five bonus points are awarded to any driver who leads the race. The driver who leads the most laps in an event receives another five bonus points. If a driver does not start the race, he will receive no points. If a driver starts the race and turns the car over to a relief driver once the race has started, however, the points are awarded to the driver that started the race. In case of a tie in points, the driver with the most wins during the year wins the tie breaker. If neither driver has a win, then the greater number of second place finishes determines the tie breaker.

Finishing Position	Points	Position	Points
1	175	23	94
2	170	24	91
3	165	25	88
4	160	26	85
5	155	27	82
6	150	28	79
7	146	29	76
8	142	30	73
9	138	31	70
10	134	32	67
11	130	33	64
12	127	34	61
13	124	35	58
14	121	36	55
15	118	37	52
16	115	38	49
17	112	39	46
18	109	40	43
19	106	41	40
20	103	42	37
21	100	43	34
22	97		

TRACKS

ATLANTA MOTOR SPEEDWAY

Area	Length	Banking
Total Track	1.522 mi	
Front Straight	1,320 ft	5 deg
Turn 1	1,349 ft	24 deg
Turn 2	1,349 ft	24 deg
Back Straight	1,320 ft	5 deg
Turn 3	1,349 ft	24 deg
Turn 4	1,349 ft	24 deg

Pit Road Layout: All on front
First Winston Cup Race: 1960
Qualifying Record: 197.478 mph (Geoff Bodine 1997)
Fastest Race: 185.887 mph (Bobby Labonte 1997)
Slowest Race: 101.983 mph (Fred Lorenzen 1962)

Top Atlanta Performers

		Starts	Wins	Percent	Top 5	Percent	Top 10	Percent	Winnings
1	Dale Earnhardt	39	8	20.5	24	61.5	27	69.2	$1,392,120
2	Bill Elliot	42	5	11.9	12	28.6	17	40.5	898,165
3	Darrell Waltrip	51	3	5.9	18	35.3	28	54.9	791,235
4	Rusty Wallace	29	2	6.9	7	24.1	13	44.8	707,575
5	Morgan Shepherd	32	3	9.4	8	25.0	18	56.3	644,975
6	Terry Labonte	39	0	0.0	9	23.1	22	56.4	644,630
7	Bobby Labonte	10	2	20.0	4	40.0	5	50.0	635,430
8	Ricky Rudd	40	2	5.0	7	17.5	20	50.0	632,435
9	Mark Martin	23	2	8.7	5	21.7	11	47.8	607,240
10	Geoff Bodine	31	0	0.0	4	12.9	9	29.0	565,105
11	Ernie Irvan	18	1	5.6	6	33.3	8	44.4	532,512
12	Dale Jarrett	20	1	5.0	5	25.0	9	45.0	521,185
13	Sterling Marlin	28	0	0.0	3	10.7	10	35.7	473,220
14	Richard Petty	65	6	9.2	22	33.8	33	50.8	463,990
15	Cale Yarborough	46	7	15.2	23	50.0	29	63.0	452,255
16	Ken Schrader	27	1	3.7	3	11.1	6	22.2	441,265
17	Bobby Allison	48	5	10.4	17	35.4	27	56.3	430,230
18	Jeff Gordon	11	1	9.1	4	36.4	5	45.5	422,720
19	Kyle Petty	35	0	0.0	2	5.7	10	28.6	406,435
20	Harry Gant	32	0	0.0	5	15.6	9	28.1	396,275

TRACKS

BRISTOL MOTOR SPEEDWAY

Area	Length	Banking
Total Track	.533 mi	
Front Straight	650 ft	16 deg
Turn 1	379 ft	36 deg
Turn 2	379 ft	36 deg
Back Straight	650 ft	16 deg
Turn 3	379 ft	36 deg
Turn 4	379 ft	36 deg

Pit Road Layout: Front and back
First Winston Cup Race: 1961
Qualifying Record: 125.093 (Mark Martin 1995)
Fastest Race: 101.074 mph (Charlie Glotzbach 1971)
Slowest Race: 61.826 mph (Ned Jarrett 1965)

Top Bristol Performers

		Starts	Wins	Percent	Top 5	Percent	Top 10	Percent	Winnings
1	Dale Earnhardt	37	9	24.3	18	48.6	26	70.3	$950,971
2	Darrell Waltrip	46	12	26.1	26	56.5	32	69.6	855,675
3	Rusty Wallace	28	6	21.4	14	50.0	19	67.9	810,010
4	Terry Labonte	38	2	5.3	17	44.7	28	73.7	630,595
5	Mark Martin	22	1	4.5	12	54.5	15	68.2	586,930
6	Ricky Rudd	39	0	0.0	11	28.2	23	59.0	531,681
7	Geoff Bodine	31	0	0.0	6	19.4	10	32.3	443,896
8	Dale Jarrett	22	1	4.5	5	22.7	10	45.5	437,190
9	Bill Elliot	29	1	3.4	6	20.7	13	44.8	436,470
10	Jeff Gordon	10	3	30.0	4	40.0	5	50.0	404,900
11	Ken Schrader	26	0	0.0	4	15.4	9	34.6	389,905
12	Sterling Marlin	26	0	0.0	2	7.7	10	38.5	365,651
13	Ernie Irvan	17	1	5.9	2	11.8	2	11.8	311,395
14	Morgan Shepherd	29	0	0.0	4	13.8	11	37.9	306,776
15	Kyle Petty	30	0	0.0	2	6.7	7	23.3	299,776
16	Brett Bodine	20	0	0.0	0	0.0	5	25.0	298,192
17	Harry Gant	31	0	0.0	6	19.4	16	51.6	287,925
18	Michael Waltrip	24	0	0.0	1	4.2	6	25.0	280,447
19	Richard Petty	60	3	5.0	26	43.3	37	61.7	280,435
20	Alan Kulwicki	14	2	14.3	6	42.9	8	57.1	271,140

TRACKS

CALIFORNIA SPEEDWAY

Area	Length	Banking
Total Track	2.0 mi	
Front Straight	n/a	11 deg
Turn 1	n/a	14 deg
Turn 2	n/a	14 deg
Back Straight	n/a	3 deg
Turn 3	n/a	14 deg
Turn 4	n/a	14 deg

Pit Road Layout: All on front
First Winston Cup Race: 1997
Qualifying Record: 183.753 (Greg Sacks 1997)
Fastest Race: 155.012 mph (Jeff Gordon 1997)

Top California Performers

		Starts	Wins	Percent	Top 5	Percent	Top 10	Percent	Winnings
1	Jeff Gordon	1	1	100.0	1	100.0	1	100.0	$144,600
2	Terry Labonte	1	0	0.0	1	100.0	1	100.0	100,825
3	Ricky Rudd	1	0	0.0	1	100.0	1	100.0	78,525
4	Ted Musgrave	1	0	0.0	1	100.0	1	100.0	64,975
5	Jimmy Spencer	1	0	0.0	1	100.0	1	100.0	54,775
6	Bobby Labonte	1	0	0.0	0	0.0	1	100.0	48,950
7	Jeff Green	1	0	0.0	0	0.0	1	100.0	38,450
8	Dale Jarrett	1	0	0.0	0	0.0	1	100.0	58,750
9	Ricky Craven	1	0	0.0	0	0.0	1	100.0	42,350
10	Mark Martin	1	0	0.0	0	0.0	1	100.0	48,450
11	Michael Waltrip	1	0	0.0	0	0.0	0	0.0	40,275
12	Jeremy Mayfield	1	0	0.0	0	0.0	0	0.0	32,175
13	Johnny Benson	1	0	0.0	0	0.0	0	0.0	38,075
14	Rusty Wallace	1	0	0.0	0	0.0	0	0.0	42,975
15	Darrell Waltrip	1	0	0.0	0	0.0	0	0.0	37,725
16	Dale Earnhardt	1	0	0.0	0	0.0	0	0.0	41,975
17	Steve Grissom	1	0	0.0	0	0.0	0	0.0	36,175
18	Joe Nemechek	1	0	0.0	0	0.0	0	0.0	40,375
19	Chad Little	1	0	0.0	0	0.0	0	0.0	28,575
20	Lake Speed	1	0	0.0	0	0.0	0	0.0	29,325

TRACKS

CHARLOTTE MOTOR SPEEDWAY

Area	Length	Banking
Total Track	1.5 mi	
Front Straight	1,152 ft	5 deg
Turn 1	1,152 ft	24 deg
Turn 2	1,953 ft	24 deg
Back Straight	1,360 ft	5 deg
Turn 3	1,152 ft	24 deg
Turn 4	1,152 ft	24 deg

Pit Road Layout: All on front
First Winston Cup Race: 1960
Qualifying Record: 184.759 mph (Ward Burton 1994)
Fastest Race: 154.537 mph (Ernie Irvan 1993)
Slowest Race: 104.207 mph (Buddy Baker 1968)

Top Charlotte Performers

		Starts	Wins	Percent	Top 5	Percent	Top 10	Percent	Winnings
1	Dale Earnhardt	42	5	11.9	15	35.7	19	45.2	$1,587,238
2	Darrell Waltrip	50	6	12.0	19	38.0	29	58.0	1,182,177
3	Bill Elliot	42	2	4.8	11	26.2	21	50.0	1,154,306
4	Terry Labonte	39	1	2.6	8	20.5	18	46.2	94,580
5	Mark Martin	24	2	8.3	8	33.3	11	45.8	940,380
6	Rusty Wallace	32	2	6.3	6	18.8	14	43.8	934,900
7	Jeff Gordon	10	2	20.0	6	60.0	6	60.0	880,390
8	Dale Jarrett	22	3	13.6	8	36.4	9	40.9	859,455
9	Ricky Rudd	43	0	0.0	7	16.3	22	51.2	788,415
10	Ken Schrader	27	1	3.7	6	22.2	10	37.0	778,596
11	Geoff Bodine	28	1	3.6	5	17.9	11	39.3	763,430
12	Harry Gant	40	1	2.5	11	27.5	14	35.0	739,820
13	Bobby Allison	46	6	13.0	23	50.0	26	56.5	732,864
14	Kyle Petty	36	1	2.8	5	13.9	11	30.6	660,725
15	Richard Petty	63	4	6.3	22	34.9	30	47.6	647,648
16	Sterling Marlin	34	0	0.0	6	17.6	10	29.4	628,560
17	Morgan Shepherd	36	0	0.0	3	8.3	12	33.3	585,280
18	Ernie Irvan	16	1	6.3	5	31.3	8	50.0	579,700
19	Davey Allison	14	2	14.3	6	42.9	7	50.0	541,215
20	Michael Waltrip	26	0	0.0	3	11.5	6	23.1	483,930

TRACKS

DARLINGTON RACEWAY

Area	Length	Banking
Total Track	1.366 mi	
Front Straight	1,228 ft	2 deg
Turn 1	n/a	23 deg
Turn 2	n/a	23 deg
Back Straight	1,228 ft	2 deg
Turn 3	n/a	25 deg
Turn 4	n/a	25 deg

Pit Road Layout: All on front
First Winston Cup Race: 1960
Qualifying Record: 174.797 mph (Ward Burton 1996)
Fastest Race: 139.958 mph (Dale Earnhardt 1993)
Slowest Race: 76.260 mph (Johnny Mantz 1950)

Top Darlington Performers

		Starts	Wins	Percent	Top 5	Percent	Top 10	Percent	Winnings
1	Dale Earnhardt	38	9	23.7	16	42.1	21	55.3	$1,134,705
2	Bill Elliot	40	5	12.5	19	47.5	30	75.0	890,830
3	Darrell Waltrip	49	5	10.2	18	36.7	23	46.9	755,625
4	Mark Martin	23	1	4.3	11	47.8	16	69.6	609,211
5	Ricky Rudd	42	1	2.4	7	16.7	21	50.0	602,914
6	Terry Labonte	38	1	2.6	10	26.3	18	47.4	575,855
7	Dale Jarrett	20	1	5.0	4	20.0	6	30.0	558,084
8	Harry Gant	31	4	12.9	9	29.0	15	48.4	544,465
9	Rusty Wallace	28	0	0.0	10	35.7	15	53.6	536,805
10	Jeff Gordon	10	4	40.0	5	50.0	6	60.0	527,355
11	Geoff Bodine	32	0	0.0	3	9.4	15	46.9	502,102
12	Sterling Marlin	27	1	3.7	7	25.9	12	44.4	487,482
13	Richard Petty	66	3	4.5	25	37.9	34	51.5	477,105
14	Ken Schrader	26	0	0.0	7	26.9	10	38.5	407,435
15	Bobby Allison	45	5	11.1	14	31.1	26	57.8	387,875
16	Kyle Petty	33	0	0.0	0	0.0	5	15.2	369,650
17	Dave Marcis	55	0	0.0	9	16.4	16	29.1	351,998
18	Morgan Shepherd	32	0	0.0	3	9.4	12	37.5	346,117
19	Brett Bodine	21	0	0.0	2	9.5	5	23.8	338,245
20	David Pearson	47	10	21.3	24	51.1	30	63.8	331,885

TRACKS

Daytona International Speedway

Area	Length	Banking
Total Track	2.5 mi	
Front Straight	3,800 ft	18 deg
Turn 1	1,500 ft	31 deg
Turn 2	1,500 ft	31 deg
Back Straight	3,600 ft	6 deg
Turn 3	1,500 ft	31 deg
Turn 4	1,500 ft	31 deg

Pit Road Layout: All on front

First Winston Cup Race: 1959

Qualifying Record: 210.364 mph (Bill Elliott 1987)

Fastest Race: 177.602 mph (Buddy Baker 1980)

Slowest Race: 124.740 mph (Junior Johnson 1960)

Top Daytona Performers

		Starts	Wins	Percent	Top 5	Percent	Top 10	Percent	Winnings
1	Dale Earnhardt	39	2	5.1	18	46.2	29	74.4	$2,244,281
2	Bill Elliot	41	4	9.8	13	31.7	21	51.2	173,439
3	Sterling Marlin	31	3	9.7	11	35.5	17	54.8	1,654,515
4	Terry Labonte	38	0	0.0	10	26.3	21	55.3	1,539,050
5	Darrell Waltrip	49	1	2.0	13	26.5	18	36.7	1,412,948
6	Geoff Bodine	32	1	3.1	6	18.8	12	37.5	1,267,810
7	Ken Schrader	26	0	0.0	6	23.1	16	61.5	1,176,077
8	Dale Jarrett	21	2	9.5	6	28.6	9	42.9	1,187,965
9	Ricky Rudd	42	0	0.0	4	9.5	18	42.9	1,035,029
10	Jeff Gordon	10	2	20.0	6	60.0	7	70.0	1,023,302
11	Ernie Irvan	17	2	11.8	6	35.3	8	47.1	1,003,077
12	Bobby Allison	48	6	12.5	16	33.3	20	41.7	992,985
13	Richard Petty	64	10	15.6	23	35.9	29	45.3	984,270
14	Morgan Shepherd	32	0	0.0	6	18.8	11	34.4	93,732
15	Mark Martin	23	0	0.0	3	13.0	7	30.4	897,410
16	Cale Yarborough	48	8	16.7	17	35.4	21	43.8	871,467
17	Buddy Baker	56	2	3.6	19	33.9	27	48.2	831,377
18	Rusty Wallace	28	0	0.0	2	7.1	7	25.0	824,834
19	Kyle Petty	32	0	0.0	2	6.3	7	21.9	762,451
20	Davey Allison	14	2	14.3	4	28.6	5	35.7	719,075

TRACKS

DOVER DOWNS INTERNATIONAL SPEEDWAY

Area	Length	Banking
Total Track	1 mi	
Front Straight	1,076 ft	9 deg
Turn 1	782 ft	24 deg
Turn 2	782 ft	24 deg
Back Straight	1,076 ft	9 deg
Turn 3	782 ft	24 deg
Turn 4	782 ft	24 deg

Pit Road Layout: All on front

First Winston Cup Race: 1969

Qualifying Record: 155.086 mph (Bobby Labonte 1996)

Fastest Race: 125.945 mph (Bill Elliott 1990)

Slowest Race: 100.820 mph (David Pearson 1975)

Top Dover Performers

		Starts	Wins	Percent	Top 5	Percent	Top 10	Percent	Winnings
1	Dale Earnhardt	38	3	7.9	19	50.0	23	60.5	$964,895
2	Ricky Rudd	39	4	10.3	12	30.8	21	53.8	744,665
3	Bill Elliot	30	4	13.3	11	36.7	18	60.0	716,190
4	Mark Martin	22	1	4.5	11	50.0	12	54.5	703,115
5	Rusty Wallace	28	3	10.7	9	32.1	15	53.6	692,465
6	Darrell Waltrip	49	2	4.1	14	28.6	21	42.9	662,910
7	Ken Schrader	26	1	3.8	8	30.8	14	53.8	591,460
8	Jeff Gordon	10	3	30.0	4	40.0	6	60.0	563,490
9	Terry Labonte	38	0	0.0	8	21.1	13	34.2	563,150
10	Kyle Petty	33	1	3.0	7	21.2	13	39.4	536,745
11	Geoff Bodine	31	1	3.2	5	16.1	9	29.0	535,620
12	Harry Gant	31	4	12.9	10	32.3	13	41.9	519,940
13	Morgan Shepherd	32	0	0.0	3	9.4	14	43.8	415,070
14	Dale Jarrett	22	0	0.0	4	18.2	5	22.7	395,560
15	Richard Petty	46	7	15.2	16	34.8	26	56.5	387,655
16	Bobby Allison	35	7	20.0	18	51.4	25	71.4	372,070
17	Ernie Irvan	17	0	0.0	4	23.5	6	35.3	347,300
18	Dave Marcis	49	0	0.0	5	10.2	14	28.6	343,600
19	Michael Waltrip	24	0	0.0	4	16.7	7	29.2	338,915
20	Bobby Labonte	10	0	0.0	4	40.0	6	60.0	320,215

TRACKS

INDIANAPOLIS MOTOR SPEEDWAY

Area	Length	Banking
Total Track	2.5 mi	
Front Straight	3,300 ft	0 deg
Turn 1	1,650 ft	9 deg
Turn 2	1,650 ft	9 deg
Back Straight	3,300 ft	0 deg
Turn 3	1,650 ft	9 deg
Turn 4	1,650 ft	9 deg

Pit Road Layout: All on front
First Winston Cup Race: 1994
Qualifying Record: 177.763 mph (Ernie Irvan 1997)
Fastest Race: 155.206 mph (Dale Earnhardt 1995)
Slowest Race: 130.814 mph (Ricky Rudd 1997)

Top Indianapolis Performers

		Starts	Wins	Percent	Top 5	Percent	Top 10	Percent	Winnings
1	Jeff Gordon	4	1	25.0	2	50.0	3	75.0	$1,273,466
2	Dale Jarrett	4	1	25.0	3	75.0	3	75.0	1,024,360
3	Dale Earnhardt	4	1	25.0	2	50.0	2	50.0	847,995
4	Ricky Rudd	4	1	25.0	1	25.0	2	50.0	819,935
5	Bill Elliot	4	0	0.0	2	50.0	4	100.0	597,345
6	Rusty Wallace	4	0	0.0	2	50.0	3	75.0	576,840
7	Mark Martin	4	0	0.0	2	50.0	2	50.0	500,345
8	Ernie Irvan	4	0	0.0	1	25.0	2	50.0	460,845
9	Bobby Labonte	4	0	0.0	0	0.0	1	25.0	458,535
10	Terry Labonte	4	0	0.0	1	25.0	1	25.0	425,290
11	Brett Bodine	4	0	0.0	1	25.0	2	50.0	419,395
12	Rick Mast	4	0	0.0	0	0.0	1	25.0	377,720
13	Ken Schrader	4	0	0.0	0	0.0	1	25.0	319,275
14	Sterling Marlin	4	0	0.0	0	0.0	1	25.0	307,835
15	Morgan Shepherd	3	0	0.0	1	33.3	3	100.0	301,485
16	Jeff Burton	4	0	0.0	0	0.0	0	0.0	296,090
17	Darrell Waltrip	4	0	0.0	0	0.0	1	25.0	295,165
18	Johnny Benson	2	0	0.0	0	0.0	2	100.0	288,245
19	Jeremy Mayfield	4	0	0.0	1	25.0	1	25.0	283,980
20	Michael Waltrip	4	0	0.0	0	0.0	1	25.0	271,790

TRACKS

MARTINSVILLE SPEEDWAY

Area	Length	Banking
Total Track	0.526 mi	
Front Straight	800 ft	0 deg
Turn 1	295 ft	12 deg
Turn 2	295 ft	12 deg
Back Straight	800 ft	0 deg
Turn 3	295 ft	12 deg
Turn 4	295 ft	12 deg

Pit Road Layout: Front and back
First Winston Cup Race: 1956
Qualifying Record: 94.129 mph (Ted Musgrave 1994)
Fastest Race: 82.223 mph (Jeff Gordon 1996)
Slowest Race: 56.440 mph (Lee Petty 1959)

Top Martinsville Performers

		Starts	Wins	Percent	Top 5	Percent	Top 10	Percent	Winnings
1	Darrell Waltrip	46	11	23.9	27	58.7	31	67.4	$939,100
2	Dale Earnhardt	38	6	15.8	15	39.5	20	52.6	893,180
3	Rusty Wallace	28	6	21.4	14	50.0	16	57.1	881,345
4	Geoff Bodine	33	4	12.1	10	30.3	12	36.4	653,665
5	Terry Labonte	39	0	0.0	12	30.8	24	61.5	564,205
6	Ricky Rudd	37	2	5.4	9	24.3	14	37.8	511,225
7	Mark Martin	24	1	4.2	7	29.2	14	58.3	472,540
8	Harry Gant	32	3	9.4	13	40.6	17	53.1	447,382
9	Bill Elliot	30	0	0.0	3	10.0	11	36.7	413,340
10	Jeff Gordon	10	2	20.0	5	50.0	7	70.0	409,435
11	Kyle Petty	35	0	0.0	5	14.3	12	34.3	363,015
12	Ernie Irvan	16	1	6.3	4	25.0	6	37.5	361,310
13	Richard Petty	66	15	22.7	30	45.5	37	56.1	353,243
14	Ken Schrader	26	0	0.0	1	3.8	15	57.7	345,805
15	Dale Jarrett	22	0	0.0	4	18.2	8	36.4	312,160
16	Morgan Shepherd	32	1	3.1	4	12.5	7	21.9	307,325
17	Brett Bodine	18	0	0.0	4	22.2	9	50.0	298,932
18	Bobby Allison	44	0	0.0	17	38.6	28	63.6	233,746
19	Rick Mast	17	0	0.0	1	5.9	2	11.8	227,405
20	Dave Marcis	52	1	1.9	8	15.4	15	28.8	226,211

TRACKS

MICHIGAN SPEEDWAY

Area	Length	Banking
Total Track	2 mi	
Front Straight	3,600 ft	12 deg
Turn 1	1,180 ft	18 deg
Turn 2	1,180 ft	18 deg
Back Straight	2,242 ft	5 deg
Turn 3	1,180 ft	18 deg
Turn 4	1,180 ft	18 deg

Pit Road Layout: All on front
First Winston Cup Race: 1969
Qualifying Record: 186.611 mph (Jeff Gordon 1995)
Fastest Race: 166.033 mph (Rusty Wallace 1996)
Slowest Race: 107.583 mph (Richard Petty 1975)

Top Michigan Performers

		Starts	Wins	Percent	Top 5	Percent	Top 10	Percent	Winnings
1	Bill Elliot	40	7	17.5	16	40.0	25	62.5	$1,001,983
2	Dale Earnhardt	36	2	5.6	10	27.8	22	61.1	847,053
3	Rusty Wallace	28	4	14.3	14	50.0	17	60.7	831,960
4	Darrell Waltrip	45	2	4.4	17	37.8	25	55.6	802,483
5	Mark Martin	24	3	12.5	10	41.7	16	66.7	758,940
6	Ricky Rudd	42	1	2.4	7	16.7	18	42.9	660,002
7	Terry Labonte	38	0	0.0	7	18.4	12	31.6	656,250
8	Geoff Bodine	31	1	3.2	6	19.4	11	35.5	620,535
9	Dale Jarrett	20	2	10.0	5	25.0	10	50.0	530,758
10	Davey Allison	13	3	23.1	7	53.8	9	69.2	510,605
11	Harry Gant	31	1	3.2	10	32.3	17	54.8	478,880
12	Morgan Shepherd	32	0	0.0	6	18.8	12	37.5	477,145
13	Ernie Irvan	17	1	5.9	8	47.1	9	52.9	462,045
14	Jeff Gordon	10	0	0.0	7	70.0	8	80.0	461,193
15	Kyle Petty	33	0	0.0	3	9.1	9	27.3	432,325
16	Ken Schrader	27	0	0.0	0	0.0	5	18.5	429,935
17	Sterling Marlin	23	0	0.0	2	8.7	6	26.1	425,380
18	Bobby Labonte	10	2	20.0	3	30.0	7	70.0	404,570
19	Dave Marcis	55	0	0.0	6	10.9	13	23.6	338,192
20	Bobby Allison	37	4	10.8	16	43.2	24	64.9	330,450

New Hampshire International Speedway

Area	Length	Banking
Total Track	1.058 mi	
Front Straight	1500 ft	0 deg
Turn 1	647 ft	12 deg
Turn 2	647 ft	12 deg
Back Straight	1500 ft	5 deg
Turn 3	647 ft	12 deg
Turn 4	647 ft	12 deg

Pit Road Layout: 42 Pits - All on front
First Winston Cup Race: 1993
Qualifying Record: 129.423 mph (Ken Schrader 1997)
Fastest Race: 117.134 mph (Jeff Burton 1997)
Slowest Race: 87.599 mph (Ricky Rudd 1994)

Top New Hampshire Performers

		Starts	Wins	Percent	Top 5	Percent	Top 10	Percent	Winnings
1	Jeff Gordon	6	2	33.3	2	33.3	3	50.0	$464,065
2	Ernie Irvan	5	1	20.0	2	40.0	3	60.0	316,325
3	Dale Earnhardt	6	0	0.0	2	33.3	3	50.0	290,850
4	Mark Martin	6	0	0.0	4	66.7	5	83.3	284,325
5	Ricky Rudd	6	1	16.7	4	66.7	5	83.3	277,925
6	Rusty Wallace	6	1	16.7	3	50.0	5	83.3	276,625
7	Dale Jarrett	6	0	0.0	1	16.7	3	50.0	248,300
8	Jeff Burton	4	1	25.0	1	25.0	2	50.0	230,850
9	Terry Labonte	6	0	0.0	1	16.7	3	50.0	208,358
10	Sterling Marlin	6	0	0.0	0	0.0	3	50.0	183,700
11	Bobby Hamilton	5	0	0.0	1	20.0	1	20.0	181,875
12	Bobby Labonte	6	0	0.0	0	0.0	1	16.7	175,900
13	Geoff Bodine	6	0	0.0	0	0.0	1	16.7	168,400
14	Ken Schrader	6	0	0.0	0	0.0	1	16.7	164,800
15	Jimmy Spencer	6	0	0.0	0	0.0	1	16.7	157,950
16	Rick Mast	6	0	0.0	0	0.0	1	16.7	154,375
17	Bill Elliot	6	0	0.0	0	0.0	2	33.3	152,650
18	Ted Musgrave	6	0	0.0	0	0.0	1	16.7	148,700
19	Brett Bodine	6	0	0.0	0	0.0	0	0.0	147,100
20	Hut Stricklin	6	0	0.0	0	0.0	1	16.7	143,375

TRACKS

NORTH CAROLINA SPEEDWAY (ROCKINGHAM)

Area	Length	Banking
Total Track	1.017 mi	
Front Straight	1,005 ft	8 deg
Turn 1	676 ft	22 deg
Turn 2	676 ft	22 deg
Back Straight	1,030 ft	8 deg
Turn 3	676 ft	25 deg
Turn 4	676 ft	25 deg

Pit Road Layout: All on front
First Winston Cup Race: 1965
Qualifying Record: 157.885 mph (Mark Martin 1997)
Fastest Race: 130.748 mph (Kyle Petty 1992)
Slowest Race: 97.865 mph (Richard Petty 1977)

Top Rockingham Performers

		Starts	Wins	Percent	Top 5	Percent	Top 10	Percent	Winnings
1	Kyle Petty	35	3	8.6	4	11.4	12	34.3	$951,662
2	Dale Earnhardt	38	3	7.9	12	31.6	26	68.4	894,765
3	Darrell Waltrip	50	4	8.0	19	38.0	29	58.0	698,895
4	Rusty Wallace	28	5	17.9	8	28.6	13	46.4	693,535
5	Terry Labonte	38	2	5.3	13	34.2	22	57.9	682,375
6	Bill Elliot	36	3	8.3	11	30.6	19	52.8	661,560
7	Ricky Rudd	40	1	2.5	12	30.0	16	40.0	633,846
8	Mark Martin	23	1	4.3	7	30.4	12	52.2	508,489
9	Richard Petty	54	11	20.4	23	42.6	28	51.9	488,940
10	Geoff Bodine	31	0	0.0	5	16.1	11	35.5	488,290
11	Dale Jarrett	21	0	0.0	5	23.8	6	28.6	454,455
12	Jeff Gordon	10	2	20.0	3	30.0	3	30.0	451,995
13	Harry Gant	31	0	0.0	12	38.7	17	54.8	439,785
14	Sterling Marlin	25	0	0.0	5	20.0	10	40.0	418,542
15	Ken Schrader	26	0	0.0	6	23.1	10	38.5	414,720
16	Morgan Shepherd	32	0	0.0	6	18.8	11	34.4	383,535
17	Bobby Allison	44	4	9.1	23	52.3	27	61.4	362,310
18	Ernie Irvan	17	0	0.0	4	23.5	8	47.1	354,155
19	Michael Waltrip	24	0	0.0	1	4.2	3	12.5	302,475
20	Dave Marcis	58	0	0.0	4	6.9	14	24.1	298,965

TRACKS

PHOENIX INTERNATIONAL RACEWAY

Area	Length	Banking
Total Track	1 mi	
Front Straight	1,179 ft	0 deg
Turn 1	637.5 ft	11 deg
Turn 2	637.5 ft	11 deg
Back Straight	1551 ft	0 deg
Turn 3	637.5 ft	9 deg
Turn 4	637.5 ft	9 deg

Pit Road Layout: All on front
First Winston Cup Race: 1988
Qualifying Record: 131.579 mph (Bobby Hamilton 1997)
Fastest Race: 110.824 mph (Dale Jarrett 1997)
Slowest Race: 90.457 mph (Alan Kulwicki 1988)

Top Phoenix Performers

		Starts	Wins	Percent	Top 5	Percent	Top 10	Percent	Winnings
1	Mark Martin	10	1	10.0	5	50.0	8	80.0	$329,430
2	Dale Earnhardt	10	1	10.0	4	40.0	7	70.0	310,780
3	Terry Labonte	10	1	10.0	4	40.0	4	40.0	299,440
4	Rusty Wallace	10	0	0.0	4	40.0	4	40.0	254,183
5	Ricky Rudd	10	1	10.0	1	10.0	3	30.0	233,145
6	Bill Elliot	10	1	10.0	4	40.0	4	40.0	232,795
7	Dale Jarrett	10	1	10.0	2	20.0	3	30.0	232,787
8	Darrell Waltrip	10	0	0.0	4	40.0	7	70.0	299,250
9	Sterling Marlin	10	0	0.0	2	20.0	4	40.0	193,450
10	Davey Allison	5	2	40.0	3	60.0	3	60.0	192,680
11	Ken Schrader	10	0	0.0	2	20.0	4	40.0	190,248
12	Geoff Bodine	10	0	0.0	0	0.0	6	60.0	186,065
13	Bobby Hamilton	5	1	20.0	2	40.0	3	60.0	185,515
14	Ernie Irvan	9	0	0.0	1	11.1	4	44.4	173,590
15	Derrike Cope	10	0	0.0	1	10.0	2	20.0	155,230
16	Kyle Petty	10	0	0.0	1	10.0	3	30.0	151,785
17	Jeff Gordon	5	0	0.0	3	60.0	3	60.0	142,915
18	Ted Musgrave	8	0	0.0	1	12.5	3	37.5	142,553
19	Alan Kulwicki	5	1	20.0	3	60.0	4	80.0	135,425
20	Morgan Shepherd	9	0	0.0	1	11.1	3	33.3	132,887

TRACKS

POCONO RACEWAY

Area	Length	Banking
Total Track	2.5 mi	
Front Straight	3,740 ft	0 deg
Turn 1	n/a	14 deg
Long Pond Straight	3,055 ft	8 deg
Turn 2	n/a	6 deg
North Straight	1,780 ft	0 deg

Pit Road Layout: All on front
First Winston Cup Race: 1974
Qualifying Record: 169.725 mph (Jeff Gordon 1996)
Fastest Race: 144.892 mph (Rusty Wallace 1996)
Slowest Race: 111.179 mph (David Pearson 1975)

Top Pocono Performers

		Starts	Wins	Percent	Top 5	Percent	Top 10	Percent	Winnings
1	Dale Earnhardt	35	2	5.7	9	25.7	17	48.6	$762,540
2	Geoff Bodine	32	3	9.4	11	34.4	16	50.0	737,145
3	Darrell Waltrip	39	4	10.3	12	30.8	19	48.7	677,700
4	Rusty Wallace	27	3	11.1	8	29.6	11	40.7	674,442
5	Bill Elliot	30	5	16.7	12	40.0	20	66.7	654,385
6	Terry Labonte	35	2	5.7	6	17.1	15	42.9	59,985
7	Ricky Rudd	37	0	0.0	7	18.9	18	48.6	560,520
8	Mark Martin	22	0	0.0	9	40.9	15	68.2	549,195
9	Ken Schrader	26	0	0.0	6	23.1	11	42.3	505,205
10	Jeff Gordon	10	2	20.0	4	40.0	6	60.0	491,470
11	Harry Gant	28	2	7.1	14	50.0	16	57.1	490,825
12	Dale Jarrett	22	2	9.1	4	18.2	9	40.9	487,650
13	Kyle Petty	31	1	3.2	2	6.5	12	38.7	424,930
14	Sterling Marlin	25	0	0.0	2	8.0	8	32.0	378,440
15	Morgan Shepherd	29	0	0.0	5	17.2	10	34.5	374,370
16	Brett Bodine	22	0	0.0	2	9.1	9	40.9	322,750
17	Derrike Cope	20	0	0.0	0	0.0	1	5.0	318,120
18	Michael Waltrip	24	0	0.0	1	4.2	2	8.3	309,995
19	Ernie Irvan	18	0	0.0	1	5.6	3	16.7	293,835
20	Richard Petty	30	2	6.7	8	26.7	12	40.0	280,140

TRACKS

RICHMOND INTERNATIONAL RACEWAY

Area	Length	Banking
Total Track	0.75 mi	
Front Straight	n/a	8 deg
Turn 1	n/a	14 deg
Turn 2	n/a	14 deg
Back Straight	860 ft	2 deg
Turn 3	n/a	14 deg
Turn 4	n/a	14 deg

Pit Road Layout: All on front
First Winston Cup Race: 1959
Qualifying Record: 124.757 mph (Jeff Gordon 1995)
Fastest Race: 109.047 mph (Dale Jarrett 1997)
Slowest Race: 45.535 mph (Lee Petty 1953)

Top Richmond Performers

		Starts	Wins	Percent	Top 5	Percent	Top 10	Percent	Winnings
1	Dale Earnhardt	38	5	13.2	24	63.2	29	76.3	$973,905
2	Rusty Wallace	28	6	21.4	15	53.6	19	67.9	756,695
3	Bill Elliot	32	1	3.1	8	25.0	14	43.8	729,570
4	Darrell Waltrip	47	6	12.8	22	46.8	33	70.2	707,817
5	Terry Labonte	39	2	5.1	11	28.2	24	61.5	622,135
6	Ricky Rudd	38	1	2.6	15	39.5	21	55.3	610,320
7	Mark Martin	24	1	4.2	5	20.8	13	54.2	479,985
8	Geoff Bodine	30	0	0.0	7	23.3	12	40.0	468,910
9	Jeff Gordon	10	1	10.0	6	60.0	7	70.0	420,870
10	Dale Jarrett	20	1	5.0	6	30.0	7	35.0	413,440
11	Kyle Petty	33	1	3.0	3	9.1	11	33.3	379,765
12	Ernie Irvan	16	2	12.5	3	18.8	4	25.0	370,025
13	Harry Gant	31	1	3.2	7	22.6	16	51.6	349,995
14	Sterling Marlin	24	0	0.0	2	8.3	5	20.8	324,490
15	Richard Petty	63	13	20.6	34	54.0	41	65.1	309,510
16	Ken Schrader	24	0	0.0	1	4.2	7	29.2	305,025
17	Bobby Allison	38	7	18.4	23	60.5	28	73.7	289,780
18	Davey Allison	11	2	18.2	5	45.5	6	54.5	283,767
19	Brett Bodine	20	0	0.0	1	5.0	4	20.0	271,950
20	Bobby Hamilton	13	0	0.0	2	15.4	5	38.5	232,160

TRACKS

SEARS POINT RACEWAY

Area	Length	Banking
Total Track:	2.52 mi	

Layout: Road Course
10 Turns of various lengths and banking.

Pit Road Layout: Front straight and island
First Winston Cup Race: 1989
Qualifying Record: 92.807 mph (Mark Martin 1997)
Fastest Race: 81.42 mph (Ernie Irvan 1992)
Slowest Race: 69.245 mph (Rusty Wallace 1990)

Top Sears Point Performers

		Starts	Wins	Percent	Top 5	Percent	Top 10	Percent	Winnings
1	Mark Martin	9	1	11.1	5	55.6	7	77.8	$366,790
2	Rusty Wallace	9	1	11.1	5	55.6	6	66.7	325,790
3	Ricky Rudd	9	1	11.1	6	66.7	7	77.8	314,400
4	Dale Earnhardt	9	1	11.1	4	44.4	7	77.8	293,925
5	Ernie Irvan	8	2	25.0	4	50.0	6	75.0	84,575
6	Terry Labonte	9	0	0.0	4	44.4	5	55.6	243,105
7	Geoff Bodine	9	1	11.1	3	33.3	5	55.6	238,755
8	Ken Schrader	9	0	0.0	2	22.2	6	66.7	182,220
9	Jeff Gordon	5	0	0.0	2	40.0	3	60.0	178,725
10	Bill Elliot	8	0	0.0	2	25.0	2	25.0	160,035
11	Sterling Marlin	9	0	0.0	0	0.0	2	22.2	158,745
12	Dale Jarrett	9	0	0.0	1	11.1	1	11.1	153,035
13	Darrell Waltrip	9	0	0.0	1	11.1	2	22.2	151,680
14	Brett Bodine	9	0	0.0	0	0.0	1	11.1	148,700
15	Michael Waltrip	9	0	0.0	0	0.0	5	55.6	146,895
16	Morgan Shepherd	9	0	0.0	0	0.0	2	22.2	144,460
17	Wally Dallenbach	6	0	0.0	2	33.3	3	50.0	133,900
18	Ted Musgrave	7	0	0.0	0	0.0	2	28.6	128,010
19	Davey Allison	8	1	12.5	1	12.5	2	25.0	120,870
20	Hut Stricklin	9	0	0.0	0	0.0	1	11.1	119,96

TRACKS

TALLADEGA SUPER SPEEDWAY

Area	Length	Banking
Total Track	2.66 mi	
Front Straight	4,300 ft	18 deg
Turn 1	1,437 ft	33 deg
Turn 2	1,437 ft	33 deg
Back Straight	4,000 ft	0 deg
Turn 3	1,437 ft	33 deg
Turn 4	1,437 ft	33 deg

Pit Road Layout: 42 Pits - All on front
First Winston Cup Race: 1969
Qualifying Record: 212.809 mph (Bill Elliott 1987)
Fastest Race: 188.354 mph (Mark Martin 1997)
Slowest Race: 130.220 mph (David Pearson 1974)

Top Talladega Performers

		Starts	Wins	Percent	Top 5	Percent	Top 10	Percent	Winnings
1	Dale Earnhardt	38	7	18.4	19	50.0	23	60.5	$1,505,260
2	Darrell Waltrip	50	4	8.0	14	28.0	18	36.0	907,840
3	Bill Elliot	42	2	4.8	10	23.8	21	50.0	907,447
4	Terry Labonte	38	2	5.3	10	26.3	18	47.4	877,512
5	Sterling Marlin	29	2	6.9	9	31.0	12	41.4	845,455
6	Mark Martin	24	2	8.3	8	33.3	15	62.5	735,506
7	Jeff Gordon	10	1	10.0	3	30.0	4	40.0	670,150
8	Ernie Irvan	18	2	11.1	9	50.0	11	61.1	642,390
9	Ricky Rudd	42	0	0.0	8	19.0	11	26.2	595,257
10	Geoff Bodine	32	0	0.0	2	6.3	7	21.9	577,970
11	Ken Schrader	26	1	3.8	5	19.2	9	34.6	552,960
12	Kyle Petty	34	0	0.0	4	11.8	15	44.1	552,310
13	Morgan Shepherd	31	0	0.0	4	12.9	13	41.9	541,485
14	Bobby Allison	37	4	10.8	13	35.1	18	48.6	519,845
15	Rusty Wallace	28	0	0.0	1	3.6	9	32.1	506,759
16	Davey Allison	14	3	21.4	5	35.7	9	64.3	496,685
17	Buddy Baker	43	4	9.3	15	34.9	20	46.5	481,085
18	Dale Jarrett	19	0	0.0	5	26.3	7	36.8	480,000
19	Harry Gant	32	1	3.1	6	18.8	12	37.5	452,595
20	Richard Petty	46	2	4.3	12	26.1	18	39.1	447,50

TRACKS

TEXAS MOTOR SPEEDWAY

Area	Length	Banking
Total Track	1.5 mi	
Front Straight	n/a	n/a
Turn 1	n/a	24 deg
Turn 2	n/a	24 deg
Back Straight	860 ft	n/a
Turn 3	n/a	24 deg
Turn 4	n/a	24 deg

Pit Road Layout: All on front
First Winston Cup Race: 1997
Qualifying Record:
Fastest Race: 125.111 mph (Jeff Burton 1997)

Top Texas Performers

		Starts	Wins	Percent	Top 5	Percent	Top 10	Percent	Winnings
1	Jeff Burton	1	1	100.0	1	100.0	1	100.0	$354,350
2	Dale Jarrett	1	0	0.0	1	100.0	1	100.0	232,800
3	Bobby Labonte	1	0	0.0	1	100.0	1	100.0	174,500
4	Terry Labonte	1	0	0.0	1	100.0	1	100.0	170,600
5	Ricky Rudd	1	0	0.0	1	100.0	1	100.0	118,775
6	Dale Earnhardt	1	0	0.0	0	0.0	1	100.0	1,117,000
7	Ward Burton	1	0	0.0	0	0.0	1	100.0	89,000
8	Sterling Marlin	1	0	0.0	0	0.0	1	100.0	93,000
9	Michael Waltrip	1	0	0.0	0	0.0	1	100.0	87,000
10	Steve Grissom	1	0	0.0	0	0.0	1	100.0	89,800
11	Bill Elliot	1	0	0.0	0	0.0	0	0.0	82,400
12	John Andretti	1	0	0.0	0	0.0	0	0.0	80,300
13	Kenny Wallace	1	0	0.0	0	0.0	0	0.0	78,200
14	Geoff Bodine	1	0	0.0	0	0.0	0	0.0	76,100
15	Dave Marcis	1	0	0.0	0	0.0	0	0.0	67,000
16	Lake Speed	1	0	0.0	0	0.0	0	0.0	72,800
17	Mike Wallace	1	0	0.0	0	0.0	0	0.0	63,000
18	Ken Schrader	1	0	0.0	0	0.0	0	0.0	70,700
19	Brett Bodine	1	0	0.0	0	0.0	0	0.0	69,600
20	Bobby Hamilton	1	0	0.0	0	0.0	0	0.0	75,540

TRACKS

WATKINS GLEN INTERNATIONAL

Area	Length	Banking
Total Track:	2.454 mi	

Road Course
11 Turns of various lengths, and banking from 6 to 10 degrees.
Front Straight: 2150 feet
Back Straight: 2600 feet
Pit Road Layout: 40 on front straight.
First Winston Cup Race: 1957
Qualifying Record: 120.733 mph (Dale Earnhardt 1996)
Fastest Race: 103.300 mph (Mark Martin 1995)
Slowest Race: 74.096 mph (Ricky Rudd 1988)

Top Watkins Glen Performers

		Starts	Wins	Percent	Top 5	Percent	Top 10	Percent	Winnings
1	Mark Martin	10	3	30.0	9	90.0	9	90.0	$543,985
2	Rusty Wallace	12	2	16.7	5	41.7	7	58.3	338,315
3	Dale Earnhardt	12	0	0.0	3	25.0	8	66.7	326,455
4	Ricky Rudd	12	2	16.7	6	50.0	7	58.3	318,060
5	Geoff Bodine	12	1	8.3	3	25.0	4	33.3	312,765
6	Terry Labonte	12	0	0.0	3	25.0	6	50.0	258,500
7	Jeff Gordon	5	1	20.0	3	60.0	4	80.0	252,935
8	Ernie Irvan	9	1	11.1	3	33.3	3	33.3	219,205
9	Bill Elliot	11	0	0.0	3	27.3	5	45.5	202,865
10	Darrell Waltrip	11	0	0.0	1	9.1	4	36.4	191,765
11	Morgan Shepherd	11	0	0.0	1	9.1	5	45.5	182,360
12	Ken Schrader	12	0	0.0	2	16.7	4	33.3	179,405
13	Kyle Petty	10	1	10.0	1	10.0	2	20.0	176,855
14	Wally Dallenbach	7	0	0.0	3	42.9	4	57.1	169,530
15	Sterling Marlin	11	0	0.0	0	0.0	3	27.3	162,695
16	Dale Jarrett	11	0	0.0	1	9.1	1	9.1	158,840
17	Michael Waltrip	12	0	0.0	1	8.3	3	25.0	157,315
18	Brett Bodine	10	0	0.0	1	10.0	2	20.0	153,520
19	Bobby Labonte	5	0	0.0	1	20.0	3	60.0	119,475
20	Ted Musgrave	7	0	0.0	1	14.3	1	14.3	116,290

A SELECT LIST OF NASCAR PRIZE MONEY WINNERS

Driver: John Andretti
Hometown: Indianapolis, IN
Birth date: March 12, 1963
Height: 5' 5"   Weight: 140
Career Starts: 126
Wins: 1   (0.80%)
Top 5's: 6   (4.80%)
Top 10's: 11   (8.80%)
Poles: 2   (1.60%)
Money Won: $2,842,613

Driver: Johnny Benson
Hometown: Grand Rapids, MI
Birth date: June 27, 1963
Height: 6'0"   Weight: 175
Career Starts: 62
Wins: 0   (0.00%)
Top 5's: 1   (1.61%)
Top 10's: 14   (22.58%)
Poles: 2   (3.23%)
Money Won: $2,203,537

Driver: Brett Bodine
Hometown: Chemung, NY
Birth date: January 11, 1959
Height: 5' 7"   Weight: 160
Career Starts: 312
Wins: 1   (0.32%)
Top 5's: 16   (5.13%)
Top 10's: 59   (18.91%)
Poles: 5   (1.34%)
Money Won: $6,061,199

Driver: Geoff Bodine
Hometown: Chemung, NY
Birth date: April 18, 1949
Height: 5' 8"   Weight: 160
Career Starts: 472
Wins: 18   (3.81%)
Top 5's: 97   (20.55%)
Top 10's: 181   (38.35%)
Poles: 37   (7.83%)
Money Won: $11,537,284

Driver: Todd Bodine
Hometown: Chemung, NY
Birth date: February 27, 1964
Height: 5' 7"   Weight: 168
Career Starts: 84
Wins: 0   (0.00%)
Top 5's: 3   (3.57%)
Top 10's: 11   (13.09%)
Poles: 1   (1.19%)
Money Won: $1,550,036

Driver: Jeff Burton
Hometown: South Boston, VA
Birth date: June 29, 1967
Height: 5' 7"   Weight: 160
Career Starts: 122
Wins: 3   (2.46%)
Top 5's: 22   (18.03%)
Top 10's: 35   (28.69%)
Poles: 1   (0.82%)
Money Won: $4,415,937

Driver: Ward Burton
Hometown: South Boston, VA
Birth date: October 25, 1961
Height: 5' 6"   Weight: 140
Career Starts: 113
Wins: 1   (0.88%)
Top 5's: 4   (3.54%)
Top 10's: 19   (16.81%)
Poles: 3   (2.65%)
Money Won: $2,917,918

Driver: Derrike Cope
Hometown: Spanaway, WA
Birth date: November 3, 1958
Height: 5' 9"   Weight: 170
Career Starts: 308
Wins: 2   (0.65%)
Top 5's: 6   (1.95%)
Top 10's: 32   (10.39%)
Poles: 1   (.32%)
Money Won: $4,447,722

Driver: Ricky Craven
Hometown: Newburgh, ME
Birth date: May 24, 1966
Height: 5' 11"   Weight: 165
Career Starts: 92
Wins: 0   (0.00%)
Top 5's: 7   (7.61%)
Top 10's: 16   (17.39%)
Poles: 2   (2.17%)
Money Won: $2,802,313

Driver: Wally Dallenbach
Hometown: Basalt, CO
Birth date: May 23, 1963
Height: 5' 10"   Weight: 170
Career Starts: 138
Wins: 0   (0.00%)
Top 5's: 5   (3.62%)
Top 10's: 13   (9.42%)
Poles: 0   (0.00%)
Money Won: $2,362,477

Driver: Dale Earnhardt
Hometown: Kannapolis, NC
Birth date: April 29, 1952
Height: 6' 1"   Weight: 185
Career Starts: 574
Wins: 70   (12.20%)
Top 5's: 256   (44.60%)
Top 10's: 370   (64.46%)
Poles: 22   (3.83%)
Money Won: $30,386,380

Driver: Bill Elliott
Hometown: Dawsonville, GA
Birth date: October 8, 1955
Height: 6' 1"   Weight: 180
Career Starts: 525
Wins: 40   (7.61%)
Top 5's: 151   (23.05%)
Top 10's: 271   (51.62%)
Poles: 49   (9.33%)
Money Won: $17,864,812

Driver: Jeff Gordon
Hometown: Pittsboro, IN
Birth date: August 4, 1971
Height: 5' 7"   Weight: 150
Career Starts: 156
Wins: 29   (18.71%)
Top 5's: 74   (47.74%)
Top 10's: 95   (61.29%)
Poles: 16   (10.32%)
Money Won: $16,702,462

Driver: Steve Grissom
Hometown: Gadsden, AL
Birth date: June 26, 1963
Height: 6' 3"   Weight: 190
Career Starts: 103
Wins: 0   (0.00%)
Top 5's: 5   (4.85%)
Top 10's: 15   (14.56%)
Poles: 0   (0.00%)
Money Won: $2,215,894

Driver: Bobby Hamilton
Hometown: Nashville, TN
Birth date: May 27, 1957
Height: 5' 10"   Weight: 185
Career Starts: 200
Wins: 2   (1.00%)
Top 5's: 13   (6.50%)
Top 10's: 37   (18.50%)
Poles: 0   (0.00%)
Money Won: $4,734,153

Driver: Ernie Irvan
Hometown: Salinas, CA
Birth date: January 13, 1959
Height: 5' 9"   Weight: 180
Career Starts: 262
Wins: 15   (5.73%)
Top 5's: 68   (25.95%)
Top 10's: 108   (41.22%)
Poles: 19   (7.25%)
Money Won: $8,951,590

Drive: Dale Jarrett
Hometown: Conover, NC
Birth date: November 26, 1956
Height: 6' 2"   Weight: 215
Career Starts: 322
Wins: 15   (4.66%)
Top 5's: 71   (33.02%)
Top 10's: 116   (53.95%)
Poles: 6   (1.86%)
Money Won: $11,293,362

Driver: Bobby Labonte
Hometown: Corpus Christi, TX
Birth date: May 8, 1964
Height: 5' 8"   Weight: 165
Career Starts: 157
Wins: 5   (3.18%)
Top 5's: 22   (14.01%)
Top 10's: 54   (34.39%)
Poles: 10   (6.37%)
Money Won: $6,061,192

Driver: Terry Labonte
Hometown: Corpus Christi, TX
Birth date: November 16, 1956
Height: 5' 8"   Weight: 170
Career Starts: 574
Wins: 19   (3.31%)
Top 5's: 166   (28.92%)
Top 10's: 309   (53.83%)
Poles: 25   (4.36%)
Money Won: $16,755,547

Driver: Chad Little
Hometown: Spokane, WA
Birth date: April 29, 1963
Height: 5' 10"   Weight: 175
Career Starts: 119
Wins: 0   (0.00%)
Top 5's: 0   (0.00%)
Top 10's: 3   (2.52%)
Poles: 0   (0.00%)
Money Won: $1,259,311

Driver: Dave Marcis
Hometown: Wausau, WI
Birth date: March 1, 1941
Height: 5' 10"   Weight: 165
Career Starts: 834
Wins: 5   (0.60%)
Top 5's: 93   (11.15%)
Top 10's: 221   (26.50%)
Poles: 14   (1.68%)
Money Won: $5,477,823

Driver: Sterling Marlin
Hometown: Columbia, TN
Birth date: June 30, 1957
Height: 6' 0"   Weight: 180
Career Starts: 403
Wins: 6   (1.49%)
Top 5's: 56   (13.90%)
Top 10's: 140   (37.74%)
Poles: 9   (2.23%)
Money Won: $10,242,027

Driver: Mark Martin
Hometown: Batesville, AR
Birth date: January 9, 1959
Height: 5' 6"   Weight: 150
Career Starts: 357
Wins: 22   (6.16%)
Top 5's: 131   (42.67%)
Top 10's: 206   (57.70%)
Poles: 35   (9.80%)
Money Won: $14,450,692

Driver: Rick Mast
Hometown: Rockbridge Baths, VA.
Birth date: March 4, 1957
Height: 6' 1"   Weight: 190
Career Starts: 245
Wins: 0   (0.00%)
Top 5's: 7   (2.86%)
Top 10's: 31   (12.65%)
Poles: 3   (1.22%)
Money Won: $4,738,831

Driver: Jeremy Mayfield
Hometown: Owensboro, KY
Birth date: May 27, 1969
Height: 6' 0"   Weight: 185
Career Starts: 110
Wins: 0   (0.00%)
Top 5's: 5   (4.54%)
Top 10's: 11   (10.00%)
Poles: 1   (0.91%)
Money Won: $2,327,956

Driver: Ted Musgrave
Hometown: Franklin, WI
Birth date: December 18, 1955
Height: 6' 1"   Weight: 185
Career Starts: 216
Wins: 0   (0.00%)
Top 5's: 18   (8.33%)
Top 10's: 48   (22.22%)
Poles: 5   (2.31%)
Money Won: $5,147,660

Driver: Joe Nemechek
Hometown: Lakeland, FL
Birth date: September 26, 1963
Height: 5' 9"   Weight: 180
Career Starts: 122
Wins: 0   (0.00%)
Top 5's: 2   (1.64%)
Top 10's: 12   (9.84%)
Poles: 2   (1.64%)
Money Won: $2,273,511

Driver: Kyle Petty
Hometown: Trinity, NC
Birth date: June 2, 1960
Height: 6' 2"   Weight: 195
Career Starts: 501
Wins: 8   (1.60%)
Top 5's: 51   (10.18%)
Top 10's: 155   (30.94%)
Poles: 8   (1.60%)
Money Won: $8,861,054

Driver: Robert Pressley
Hometown: Asheville, NC
Birth date: April 8, 1959
Height: 6' 0"   Weight: 198
Career Starts: 78
Wins: 0   (0.00%)
Top 5's: 2   (2.56%)
Top 10's: 4   (5.13%)
Poles: 0   (0.00%)
Money Won: $1,680,853

Driver: Ricky Rudd
Hometown: Chesapeake, VA
Birth date: September 12, 1956
Height: 5' 9"   Weight: 170
Career Starts: 594
Wins: 19   (3.20%)
Top 5's: 149   (25.08%)
Top 10's: 293   (49.33%)
Poles: 23   (3.87%)
Money Won: $13,502,320

Driver: Ken Schrader
Hometown: Fenton, MO
Birth date: May 29, 1955
Height: 5' 10"   Weight: 190
Career Starts: 391
Wins: 4   (1.02%)
Top 5's: 61   (15.60%)
Top 10's: 152   (38.87%)
Poles: 20   (5.12%)
Money Won: $10,148,078

Driver: Morgan Shepherd
Hometown: Conover, NC
Birth date: October 12, 1941
Height: 5' 9"   Weight: 170
Career Starts: 468
Wins: 4   (0.85%)
Top 5's: 63   (13.46%)
Top 10's: 168   (35.90%)
Poles: 7   (1.50%)
Money Won: $8,064,248

Driver: Mike Skinner
Hometown: Susanville, CA
Birth date: June 6, 1957
Height: 6' 0"   Weight: 190
Career Starts: 36
Wins: 0   (0.00%)
Top 5's: 0   (0.00%)
Top 10's: 3   (8.33%)
Poles: 2   (5.56%)
Money Won: $962,769

Driver: Lake Speed
Hometown: Jackson, MS
Birth date: January 17, 1948
Height: 5' 6"   Weight: 150
Career Starts: 386
Wins: 1   (0.23%)
Top 5's: 16   (4.15%)
Top 10's: 75   (16.43%)
Poles: 0   (0.00%)
Money Won: $4,899,666

Driver: Jimmy Spencer
Hometown: Berwick, PA
Birth date: February 15, 1957
Height: 6' 1"   Weight: 225
Career Starts: 235
Wins: 2   (0.85%)
Top 5's: 15   (6.38%)
Top 10's: 45   (19.15%)
Poles: 2   (0.85%)
Money Won: $4,647,671

Driver: Hut Stricklin
Hometown: Calera, AL
Birth date: June 24, 1961
Height: 6' 1"   Weight: 185
Career Starts: 254
Wins: 0   (0.00%)
Top 5's: 8   (3.15%)
Top 10's: 27   (10.63%)
Poles: 1   (0.39%)
Money Won: $3,838,396

Driver: Dick Trickle
Hometown: Wisconsin Rapids, WI
Birth date: October 27, 1941
Height: 5' 6"   Weight: 163
Career Starts: 252
Wins: 0   (0.00%)
Top 5's: 15   (5.95%)
Top 10's: 35   (13.89%)
Poles: 1   (0.40%)
Money Won: $3,553,484

Driver: Kenny Wallace
Hometown: St. Louis, MO
Birth date: August 23, 1963
Height: 5' 10"   Weight: 162
Career Starts: 120
Wins: 0   (0.00%)
Top 5's: 1   (0.83%)
Top 10's: 10   (8.33%)
Poles: 2   (1.67%)
Money Won: $2,178,071

Driver: Rusty Wallace
Hometown: St. Louis, MO
Birth date: August 14, 1956
Height: 6' 0"   Weight: 175
Career Starts: 425
Wins: 47   (40.00%)
Top 5's: 140   (32.94)
Top 10's: 221   (52.00%)
Poles: 19   (4.47%)
Money Won: $16,125,660

Driver: Darrell Waltrip
Hometown: Franklin, TN
Birth date: February 5, 1947
Height: 6' 1"   Weight: 190
Career Starts: 720
Wins: 84   (11.67%)
Top 5's: 275   (38.19%)
Top 10's: 388   (53.89%)
Poles: 59   (8.19%)
Money Won: $16,140,730

Driver: Michael Waltrip
Hometown: Owensboro, KY
Birth date: April 30, 1963
Height: 6' 5"   Weight: 220
Career Starts: 362
Wins: 0   (0.00%)
Top 5's: 16   (4.42%)
Top 10's: 73   (20.17%)
Poles: 2   (0.55%)
Money Won: $6,516,271

NASCAR WINSTON CUP CHAMPIONS
1949–1997

Year	Car	Driver	Owner	Car	Wins	Poles	Winnings
1997	24	Jeff Gordon	Rick Hendrick	Chevrolet	10	1	$6,375,658
1996	5	Terry Labonte	Rick Hendrick	Chevrolet	2	4	4,030,648
1995	24	Jeff Gordon	Rick Hendrick	Chevrolet	7	9	4,347,343
1994	3	Dale Earnhardt	Richard Childress	Chevrolet	4	2	3,300,733
1993	3	Dale Earnhardt	Richard Childress	Chevrolet	6	2	3,353,789
1992	7	Alan Kulwicki	Alan Kulwicki	Ford	2	6	2,322,561
1991	3	Dale Earnhardt	Richard Childress	Chevrolet	4	0	2,396,685
1990	3	Dale Earnhardt	Richard Childress	Chevrolet	9	4	3,083,056
1989	27	Rusty Wallace	Raymond Beadle	Pontiac	6	4	2,247,950
1988	9	Bill Elliott	Harry Melling	Ford	6	6	1,574,639
1987	3	Dale Earnhardt	Richard Childress	Chevrolet	11	1	2,099,243
1986	3	Dale Earnhardt	Richard Childress	Chevrolet	5	1	1,783,880
1985	11	Darrell Waltrip	Junior Johnson	Chevrolet	3	4	1,318,735
1984	44	Terry Labonte	Billy Hagan	Chevrolet	2	2	713,010
1983	22	Bobby Allison	Bill Gardner	Buick	6	0	828,355
1982	11	Darrell Waltrip	Junior Johnson	Buick	12	7	873,118
1981	11	Darrell Waltrip	Junior Johnson	Buick	12	11	693,342
1980	2	Dale Earnhardt	Ros Osterlund	Chevrolet	5	0	588,926
1979	43	Richard Petty	Petty Ent.	Chevrolet	5	1	531,292
1978	11	Cale Yarborough	Junior Johnson	Oldsmobile	10	8	530,751
1977	11	Cale Yarborough	Junior Johnson	Chevrolet	9	3	477,499
1976	11	Cale Yarborough	Junior Johnson	Chevrolet	9	2	387,173
1975	43	Richard Petty	Petty Ent.	Dodge	13	3	378,865
1974	43	Richard Petty	Petty Ent.	Dodge	10	7	299,175
1973	72	Benny Parsons	L.G. DeWitt	Chevrolet	1	0	114,345
1972	43	Richard Petty	Petty Ent.	Plymouth	8	3	227,015
1971	43	Richard Petty	Petty Ent.	Plymouth	21	9	309,225
1970	71	Bobby Isaac	Nord Krauskopf	Dodge	11	13	121,470
1969	17	David Pearson	Holman-Moody	Ford	11	14	183,700
1968	17	David Pearson	Holman-Moody	Ford	16	12	118,842
1967	43	Richard Petty	Petty Ent.	Plymouth	27	18	130,275
1966	6	David Pearson	Cotton Owens	Dodge	14	7	59,205
1965	11	Ned Jarrett	Bondy Long	Ford	13	9	77,966
1964	43	Richard Petty	Petty Ent.	Plymouth	9	8	98,810
1963	8	Joe Weatherly	—	Mercury	3	6	58,110
1962	8	Joe Weatherly	Bud Moore	Pontiac	9	6	56,110
1961	11	Ned Jarrett	W.G. Holloway, Jr.	Chevrolet	1	4	27,285
1960	4	Rex White	White-Clements	Chevrolet	6	3	45,260
1959	42	Lee Petty	Petty Ent.	Plymouth	10	2	45,570
1958	42	Lee Petty	Petty Ent.	Oldsmobile	7	4	20,600
1957	87	Buck Baker	Buck Baker	Chevrolet	10	5	24,712
1956	300 B	Buck Baker	Carl Kiekhaefer	Chrysler	14	12	29,790
1955	300	Tim Flock	Carl Kiekhaefer	Chrysler	18	19	33,750
1954	42	Lee Petty	—	Chrysler	7	3	26,706
1953	92	Herb Thomas	Herb Thomas	Hudson	11	10	27,300
1952	91	Tim Flock	Ted Chester	Hudson	8	4	20,210
1951	92	Herb Thomas	Herb Thomas	Hudson	7	4	18,200
1950	60	Bill Rexford	Julian Buesink	Oldsmobile	1	0	6,175
1949	22	Red Byron	Raymond Parks	Oldsmobile	2	1	5,800

MULTIPLE WINSTON CUP CHAMPIONS

Driver	Years
Dale Earnhardt	1994, 93, 91, 90, 87, 86, 80
Richard Petty	1979, 75, 74, 72, 71, 67, 64
David Pearson	1969, 68, 66
Lee Petty	1959, 58, 54
Darrell Waltrip	1985, 82, 81
Cale Yarborough	1978, 77, 76
Buck Baker	1957, 56
Tim Flock	1955, 52
Jeff Gordon	1995, 97
Ned Jarrett	1965, 61
Herb Thomas	1953, 51
Joe Weatherly	1963, 62

TOP 10 CLOSEST WINSTON CUP CHAMPIONSHIPS

Year	Champion	Runner-Up	Point Margin
1992	Alan Kulwicki	Bill Elliott	10
1979	Richard Petty	Darrell Waltrip	11
1989	Rusty Wallace	Dale Earnhardt	12
1997	Jeff Gordon	Dale Jarrett	14
1980	Dale Earnhardt	Cale Yarborough	19
1988	Bill Elliott	Rusty Wallace	24
1990	Dale Earnhardt	Mark Martin	26
1995	Jeff Gordon	Dale Earnhardt	34
1996	Terry Labonte	Jeff Gordon	37
1983	Bobby Allison	Darrell Waltrip	47
1981	Darrell Waltrip	Bobby Allison	53
1984	Terry Labonte	Harry Gant	65
1982	Darrell Waltrip	Bobby Allison	72

WINSTON CUP CHAMPIONS AND RUNNERS-UP

Year	Champion	Runner-Up	Spread
1997	Jeff Gordon	Dale Jarrett	14
1996	Terry Labonte	Jeff Gordon	37
1995	Jeff Gordon	Dale Earnhardt	34
1994	Dale Earnhardt	Mark Martin	444
1993	Dale Earnhardt	Rusty Wallace	80
1992	Alan Kulwicki	Ricky Rudd	10
1991	Dale Earnhardt	Dale Earnhardt	195
1990	Dale Earnhardt	Mark Martin	26
1989	Rusty Wallace	Dale Earnhardt	12
1988	Bill Elliott	Rusty Wallace	24
1987	Dale Earnhardt	Bill Elliott	489
1986	Dale Earnhardt	Darrell Waltrip	288
1985	Darrell Waltrip	Bill Elliott	101
1984	Terry Labonte	Harry Gant	65
1983	Bobby Allison	Darrell Waltrip	47
1982	Darrell Waltrip	Bobby Allison	72
1981	Darrell Waltrip	Bobby Allison	53
1980	Dale Earnhardt	Cale Yarborough	19
1979	Richard Petty	Darrell Waltrip	11
1978	Cale Yarborough	Bobby Allison	474
1977	Cale Yarborough	Richard Petty	386
1976	Cale Yarborough	Richard Petty	195
1975	Richard Petty	Dave Marcis	722
1974	Richard Petty	Cale Yarborough	567.45
1973	Benny Parsons	Cale Yarborough	67.15
1972	Richard Petty	Bobby Allison	127.90

ALL-TIME WINSTON CUP RACE WINNERS
1949 through 1995

Richard Petty	200	Sterling Marlin	6	Brett Bodine	1
David Pearson	105	Alan Kulwicki	5	Buddy Shuman	1
Bobby Allison	84	Dan Gurney	5	Chuck Stevenson	1
Darrell Waltrip	84	Bobby Labonte	5	Danny Graves	1
Cale Yarborough	83	Dave Marcis	5	Danny Weinberg	1
Dale Earnhardt	70	Ralph Moody	5	Dick Brooks	1
Lee Petty	54	Billy Wade	4	Dick Passwater	1
Junior Johnson	50	Bob Flock	4	Donald Thomas	1
Ned Jarrett	50	Charlie Glotzbach	4	Earl Balmer	1
Herb Thomas	49	Eddie Gray	4	Earl Ross	1
Rusty Wallace	47	Eddie Pagan	4	Frankie Schneider	1
Buck Baker	46	Glen Wood	4	Greg Sacks	1
Bill Elliott	40	Hershel McGriff	4	Harold Kite	1
Tim Flock	40	Ken Schrader	4	Jack White	1
Bobby Isaac	37	Lloyd Dane	4	Jim Cook	1
Fireball Roberts	32	Morgan Shepherd	4	Jim Florian	1
Jeff Gordon	29	Nelson Stacy	4	Jim Hurtubise	1
Rex White	26	Parnelli Jones	4	Jim Roper	1
Fred Lorenzen	26	Pete Hamilton	4	Jody Ridley	1
Jim Paschal	25	Jeff Burton	3	Joe Eubanks	1
Joe Weatherly	24	Bill Blair	3	Joe Lee Johnson	1
Mark Martin	22	Bobby Labonte	3	John Kieper	1
Benny Parsons	21	Dick Linder	3	John Rostek	1
Jack Smith	21	Frank Mundy	3	John Soares	1
Speedy Thimpson	19	Tiny Lund	3	Johnny Allen	1
Buddy Baker	19	Al Keller	2	Johnny Mantz	1
Davey Allison	19	Billy Myers	2	Johnny Rutherford	1
Terry Labonte	19	Bobby Johns	2	June Cleveland	1
Fonty Flock	19	Danny Letner	2	Lake Speed	1
Ricky Rudd	19	Derrike Cope	2	Larry Frank	1
Geoff Bodine	18	Elmo Langley	2	Lennie Pond	1
Harry Gant	18	Emanuel Zervakis	2	Leon Sales	1
Neil Bonnett	18	Gober Sosebee	2	Lloyd Moore	1
Curtis Turner	17	Gwyn Staley	2	Lou Figaro	1
Marvin Panch	17	James Hylton	2	Mario Andretti	1
Ernie Irvan	15	Jim Pardue	2	Mark Donohue	1
Dale Jarrett	15	Jimmy Spencer	2	Marvin Burke	1
Dick Hutcherson	14	Johnny Beauchamp	2	Neil Cole	1
Lee Roy Yarbrough	14	Marvin Porter	2	Norm Nelson	1
Dick Rathmann	13	Ray Elder	2	Paul Lewis	1
Tim Richmond	13	Red Byron	2	Phil Parsons	1
Donnie Allison	10	Tom Pistone	2	Richard Brickhouse	1
Cotton Owens	9	John Andretti	1	Ron Bouchard	1
Paul Goldsmith	9	Art Watts	1	Royce Hagerty	1
Kyle Petty	8	Bill Amick	1	Sam McQuagg	1
Jim Reed	7	Bill Norton	1	Shorty Rollins	1
A. J. Foyt	7	Bill Rexford	1	Tommy Thompson	1
Bob Welborn	7	Bob Burdick	1	Wendell Scott	1
Marshall Teague	7	Bobby Courtright	1	Whitey Norman	1
Darel Dieringer	6	Bobby Hillin, Jr.	1		

WINSTON CUP ROOKIES OF THE YEAR
1958-1995

Driver	Year	Races	Wins	Poles	Top 5	Top 10	Winnings
Mike Skinner	1997	31	0	2	0	3	$900,569
Johnny Benson	1996	30	0	1	1	6	947,080
Ricky Craven	1995	31	0	0	0	4	597,054
Jeff Burton	1994	30	0	0	2	3	594,700
Jeff Gordon (a)	1993	30	0	1	7	11	765,168
Jimmy Hensley	1992	22	0	0	0	4	247,660
Bobby Hamilton	1991	28	0	0	0	4	259,105
Rob Moroso	1990	25	0	0	0	1	162,002
Dick Trickle	1989	28	0	0	6	9	343,728
Ken Bouchard	1988	24	0	0	0	1	109,410
Davey Allison	1987	22	2	5	9	10	361,060
Alan Kulwicki (b)	1986	23	0	0	1	4	94,450
Ken Schrader	1985	28	0	0	0	3	211,523
Rusty Wallace	1984	30	0	0	2	4	195,927
Sterling Marlin	1983	30	0	0	0	1	143,564
Geoff Bodine	1982	25	0	2	4	10	258,500
Ron Bouchard	1981	22	1	1	5	12	152,855
Jody Ridley	1980	31	0	0	2	18	196,617
Dale Earnhardt (d)	1979	27	1	4	11	17	264,086
Ronnie Thomas	1978	27	0	0	0	2	73,037
Ricky Rudd	1977	25	0	0	1	10	68,448
Skip Manning	1976	27	0	0	0	4	55,820
Bruce Hill	1975	26	0	0	3	11	58,138
Earl Ross	1974	21	1	0	5	10	64,830
Lennie Pond	1973	23	0	0	1	9	25,155
Larry Smith	1972	23	0	0	0	7	24,215
Walter Ballard	1971	41	0	0	3	11	25,598
Bill Dennis	1970	25	0	0	0	5	15,670
Dick Brooks	1969	28	0	0	3	12	27,532
Pete Hamilton	1968	16	0	0	3	6	8,239
Donnie Allison	1967	20	0	0	4	7	16,440
James Hylton	1966	41	0	1	20	32	29,575
Sam McQuagg	1965	15	0	0	2	5	10,555
Doug Cooper	1964	39	0	0	4	11	10,445
Billy Wade	1963	22	0	0	4	11	8,710
Tom Cox	1962	40	0	0	12	20	8,980
Woody Wilson	1961	5	0	0	0	1	2,625
David Pearson (e)	1960	22	0	1	3	7	5,030
Richard Petty (f)	1959	22	0	0	6	9	7,630
Shorty Rollins	1958	21	1	0	10	17	8,515

(a) Won 1995 Championship.
(b) Won 1992 Championship.
(c) Won 1989 Championship.
(d) Won 1980,1986,1987,1990,1991,1993,1994 Winston Cup Championships.
(e) Won 1966,1968,1969 championships.
(f) Won 1964,1967,1971,1972,1974,1975,1979 championships.

NASCAR "CROWN JEWEL" WINNERS

Year	Daytona 500	Winston Select 500	Coca-Cola 600	Southern 500
1997	Jeff Gordon	Mark Martin	Jeff Gordon	Jeff Gordon
1996	Dale Jarrett	Sterling Marlin	Dale Jarrett	Jeff Gordon
1995	Sterling Marlin	Mark Martin	Bobby Labonte	Jeff Gordon
1994	Sterling Marlin	Dale Earnhardt	Jeff Gordon	Bill Elliott
1993	Dale Jarrett	Ernie Irvan	Dale Earnhardt	Mark Martin
1992	Davey Allison	Davey Allison	Dale Earnhardt	Darrell Waltrip
1991	Ernie Irvan	Harry Gant	Davey Allison	Harry Gant
1990	Derrike Cope	Dale Earnhardt	Rusty Wallace	Dale Earnhardt
1989	Darrell Waltrip	Davey Allison	Darrell Waltrip	Dale Earnhardt
1988	Bobby Allison	Benny Parsons	Darrell Waltrip	Bill Elliott
1987	Bill Elliott	Davey Allison	Kyle Petty	Dale Earnhardt
1986	Geoff Bodine	Bobby Allison	Dale Earnhardt	Tim Richmond
1985	Bill Elliott	Bill Elliott	Darrell Waltrip	Bill Elliott
1984	Cale Yarborough	Cale Yarborough	Bobby Allison	Harry Gant
1983	Cale Yarborough	Richard Petty	Neil Bonnett	Bobby Allison
1982	Bobby Allison	Darrell Waltrip	Neil Bonnett	Cale Yarborough
1981	Richard Petty	Bobby Allison	Bobby Allison	Neil Bonnett
1980	Buddy Baker	Buddy Baker	Benny Parsons	Terry Labonte
1979	Richard Petty	Bobby Allison	Darrell Waltrip	David Pearson
1978	Bobby Allison	Cale Yarborough	Darrell Waltrip	Cale Yarborough
1977	Cale Yarborough	Darrell Waltrip	Richard Petty	David Pearson
1976 a	David Pearson	Buddy Baker	David Pearson	David Pearson
1975	Benny Parsons	Buddy Baker	Richard Petty	Bobby Allison
1974	Richard Petty	David Pearson	David Pearson	Cale Yarborough
1973	Richard Petty	David Pearson	Buddy Baker	Cale Yarborough
1972	A.J. Foyt	David Pearson	Buddy Baker	Bobby Allison
1971	Richard Petty	Donnie Allison	Bobby Allison	Bobby Allison
1970	Pete Hamilton	Pete Hamilton	Donnie Allison	Buddy Baker
1969 b	LeeRoy Yarborough	N/A	LeeRoy Yarborough	LeeRoy Yarborough

(a) David Pearson won three of the Big Four races.

(b) LeeRoy Yarborough won the NASCAR Triple Crown.

(c) Bill Elliott became the first driver to win the Winston Million. The million dollars from Winston goes to any driver who wins three of the four crown jewels of the NASCAR Winston Cup Circuit. (Initiated in 1985.)

(d) Jeff Gordon became the second driver to win the Winston Million.

N/A - There was no Winston 500 that year, as work was still being done on the Alabama International Motor Speedway.

TOP 40 200-PLUS QUALIFIERS

	Driver	Speed	Race
1	Bill Elliott	212.809	1987 Winston 500
2	Bill Elliott	212.229	1986 Winston 500
3	Bobby Allison	211.797	1987 Winston 500
4	Davey Allison	210.61	1987 Winston 500
5	Darrell Waltrip	210.471	1987 Winston 500
6	Bill Elliott	210.364	1987 Daytona 500
7	Dale Earnhardt	210.36	1987 Winston 500
8	Kyle Petty	210.346	1987 Winston 500
9	Sterling Marlin	210.194	1987 Winston 500
10	Terry Labonte	210.101	1987 Winston 500
11	Phil Parsons (tie)	209.963	1987 Winston 500
	Lake Speed (tie)	209.963	1987 Winston 500
13	Geoff Bodine	209.71	1987 Winston 500
14	Buddy Baker	209.701	1987 Winston 500
15	Bill Elliott	209.398	1985 Winston 500
16	Bobby Allison	209.274	1986 Winston 500
17	Davey Allison	209.084	1987 Daytona 500
18	Bill Elliott	209.005	1986 Talladega 500
19	Ron Bouchard	208.91	1987 Winston 500
20	Rusty Wallace	208.251	1987 Winston 500
21	Ken Schrader	208.227	1987 Daytona 500
22	Geoff Bodine	208.169	1986 Winston 500
23	Ken Schrader	208.16	1987 Winston 500
24	Bobby Hillin Jr.	208.142	1987 Winston 500
25	Ricky Rudd	208.138	1987 Winston 500
26	Cale Yarborough (tie)	208.092	1986 Winston 500
	Cale Yarborough (tie)	208.092	1987 Winston 500
28	Dale Earnhardt	208.052	1986 Talladega 500
29	Morgan Shepherd	207.831	1987 Winston 500
30	Bobby Allison	207.795	1987 Daytona 500
31	Sterling Marlin	207.776	1986 Winston 500
32	Benny Parsons	207.659	1987 Winston 500
33	Bill Elliott	207.578	1985 Talladega 500
34	Tim Richmond	207.538	1986 Talladega 500
35	Benny Parsons (tie)	207.403	1886 Talladega 500
	Neil Bonnett (tie)	207.403	1987 Winston 500
37	Morgan Shepherd	207.389	1986 Winston 500
38	Greg Sacks	207.246	1987 Winston 500
39	Sterling Marlin	207.192	1986 Talladega 500
40	Buddy Baker	207.151	1986 Winston 500

(Fifty-eight drivers have run 200 or better during their Winston Cup careers. Cale Yarborough has topped 200 15 times to lead this list.)

ALL-TIME DRIVER RECORDS
1949–1993

All Races
Most Wins, Career: 200, Richard Petty, 1958–92.
Most Wins, Season: 27, Richard Petty, 1967.
Most Consecutive Wins: 10, Richard Petty, 1967.
Most Wins from Pole, Career: 61, Richard Petty, 1958–1992.
Most Wins from Pole, Season: 15, Richard Petty, 1967.
Oldest Driver to Win a Race: Harry Gant, 52 years, 219 days (Aug. 16, 1992).
Youngest Driver to Win a Race: Donald Thomas, 20 years, 129 days (Nov. 16, 1952).
Most Consecutive Races Won from Pole, Individual: 4, Richard Petty, 1967; Darrell Waltrip, 1981.
Most Consecutive Races Won from Pole: 6, D. Pearson, J. Paschal 2, R. Petty 3, 1966.
Most Years Won at Least 1 Race from Pole: 16, Richard Petty, 1958–92.
Most Consecutive Years Won at Least 1 Race from Pole: 13, Richard Petty, 1960–72.
Most Wins at 1 Track: 15, Richard Petty, at Martinsville Speedway and North Wilkesboro Speedway.
Most Consecutive Wins at 1 Track: 7, Richard Petty, Richmond Fairgrounds Raceway, 1970–73; Darrell Waltrip, Bristol International Raceway, 1981–84.

SUPER SPEEDWAYS

Most Wins, Career: 55, Richard Petty, 1958–92.
Most Wins, Season: 11, Bill Elliott, 1985
Most Consecutive Wins: 4, Bobby Allison (twice), 1971; Richard Petty, 1971–72; David Pearson, 1973; Bill Elliott, 1985.
Oldest Driver to Win a Race: Harry Gant, 52 years, 219 days (Aug. 16, 1992).
Most Wins from Pole, Career: 20, David Pearson, 1960–86.
Most Wins from Pole, Season: 6, David Pearson, 1976; Bill Elliott, 1985.
Most Consecutive Races Won from Pole: 2, held by many; last was Bill Elliott, who did it twice in 1985.
Most Years Won at Least 1 Race from Pole: 7, Cale Yarborough, David Pearson.
Most Consecutive Years Won at Least 1 Race from Pole: 5, David Pearson, 1972–76.
Most Wins at 1 Track: 11, Richard Petty, at North Carolina Motor Speedway.
Most Consecutive Wins at 1 Track: 4, Bill Elliott, Michigan International Speedway, 1985–86

SHORT TRACKS

Most Wins, Career: 145, Richard Petty, 1958–92.
Most Wins, Season: 24, Richard Petty, 1967.
Most Consecutive Wins: 10, Richard Petty, 1967.
Most Wins from Pole, Career: 54, Richard Petty, 1958–1992.
Most Wins from Pole, Season: 14, Richard Petty, 1967.
Most Years Won at least 1 Race from Pole: 14, Richard Petty, 1958–1992.
Most Consecutive Years Won at Least 1 Race from Pole: 12, Richard Petty, 1960–71.
Most Wins at 1 Track: 15, Richard Petty, at Martinsville Speedway and North Wilkesboro Speedway.
Most Consecutive Wins at 1 Track: 7, Richard Petty, Richmond Fairgrounds Raceway, 1970–73; Darrell Waltrip, Bristol International Raceway, 1981–84.

INDEX

Body, assembling, 16–25
    Body templates, 23
Body components, 26–44
    Air dam, front, 32, 36
    Body panels, 20
    Cockpit, 40, 43
    Crush panels, 30, 32
    Deck, 17
    Deck lids, 31, 32, 35
    Doors, 18, 30–32
    Fascia, front, 17, 26, 28
    Fascia, rear, 21, 32, 36
    Fenders, 18, 31, 33, 34
    Fire extinguishing system, 40
    Firewall, 15, 29–31
    Fuel intake, 31, 34
    Gauges, 40, 43
    Grill, 26, 27
    Hood, 17, 27, 30
    Quarter panels, 18, 31, 34
    Roll bars, 16, 40, 44
    Roof, 16, 27–30
    Roof flaps, 28, 29, 31
    Roof pillars, 22
    Seat, 40, 44
    Spoiler, rear, 32–35, 37, 38
    Stickers, 25, 31, 33
    Trunk area, 20
    Windows, quarter, 37, 38, 40
    Windows, rear, 38, 42
    Windows, side, 36, 37, 40, 41
    Windshield, 34, 39
Brakes, 77–80
    Air scoops, 80
    Brake calipers, 77–79
    Brake lines, 77, 78
    Brake pads, 78, 79
    Brake rotors, 78–80
    Fans, 80
    Master cylinders, 77, 78
Building a car, 11, 12
Car specifications and rules, 10
"Crown Jewel" winners, 188
Driver records, 190
Drivetrain, 65, 66
    Clutch, 65
    Driveshaft, 66

Flywheel, 65
    Rear end gear ratio, 66
    Transmission, 65, 66
Engine, 45–64
    Air filters, 52, 53
    Alternators, 63, 64
    Battery, 63, 64
    Blocks, 45–47
    Camshafts, 48, 49
    Carburetors, 51, 52
    Collector pipes, 53, 54
    Connecting rods, 46–48
    Cooling system, 60, 61
    Crankshafts, 46, 47
    Cylinder heads, 47–49
    Engine placement, 45
    Exhaust pipes, 64–56
    Exhaust system, 52–56
    Fans, 60, 62
    Fuel cell, 62, 63
    Fuel filter, 61
    Fuel line, braided, 63
    Fuel pumps, 61–63
    Header pipes, 52–54
    Ignition system, 62, 63
    Intake manifold, 50–52
    Lifters, 49
    Oil cooler, 57–59
    Oil filters, 58–60
    Oil pan, 55
    Oil pumps, 57, 58, 60
    Oil system, 56–58
    Oil tank, 56
    Pistons, 47, 48
    Push rods, 49, 50
    Radiator, 59, 61, 62
    Radiator hoses, 61
    Restricter plates, 52
    Rocker arms, 49, 50
    Starters, 64
    Valves, 50
    Valve springs, 50
    Water pumps, 60, 62
Entry procedure, 161
Flags, 159, 160
Fuel, 135
Handling terms, 122–124

Aerodynamics, 120, 123, 124
Alignment, 123
Camber, 119, 123
Caster, 119, 123
Centrifugal force, 116
Oversteer, 118, 119, 122
Toe, 119, 123
Understeer, 118, 119, 122, 123
Hauler, 109–112
Inspection, 137–141, 161, 162
Licenses, 160, 161
NASCAR prize money winners, 182, 183
Painting, 24
Pits
    Pit equipment, 145
    Pit stall, setting up, 145
    Pit stops, 148–153
    Pit stop strategy, 150–152
Points determination, 162
Practice, 133–135
    Happy Hour, 134, 135
    Race setup, 133, 134
Qualifying, 128–132
    Engine, 128
    Order, 130
    Practice, 128, 129
    Provisional starting positions, 131
    Runs, 130, 131
    Setup, 128–130
Race day, 142–147
Race tracks, stats and top performers, 163–181
    Atlanta Motor Speedway, 163
    Bristol Motor Speedway, 164
    California Speedway, 165
    Charlotte Motor Speedway, 166
    Darlington Raceway, 167
    Daytona International Speedway, 168
    Dover Downs International Speedway, 169
    Indianapolis Motor Speedway, 170
    Martinsville Speedway, 171
    Michigan Speedway, 172
    New Hampshire International Speedway, 173
    North Carolina Speedway (Rockingham), 174
    Phoenix International Raceway, 175
    Pocono Raceway, 176
    Richmond International Raceway, 177
    Sears Point Raceway, 178

Talladega Super Speedway, 179
Texas Motor Speedway, 180
Watkins Glen International, 181
Roll cage, building the, 13–16
Floorboard, 15
Frame rails, 13
Side bars, 15
Side rails, 13
Suspension fittings, 14
Welding, 14
Setup, 113–126
Brakes, 120
Engine power, 114
Suspension , 114, 117, 120, 121
Setup adjustments, 124–126
Fender support rods, 126
Grill openings, 123, 125, 126
Spoiler, rear, 122, 125
Stagger, 123, 126
Tire pressure, 124, 126
Tire temperature, 125, 126
Wedge, 121, 124, 125
Weight distribution, 120, 121
Shop and equipment, 97–108
CNC machining equipment, 99
Computerized coordinate-measuring machines, 103
Dyno control, 102
Engine assembly room, 105

Engine testing equipment, 108
Fitness centers, 98
Mills and lathes, 100, 107
Paint room, 102
Primary assembly area, 101
Replica pit wall, 106
Sheet-metal fabrication room, 104
Spin Tron, 108
Storage space, 98, 108
Surface plates, 101
Workbench, 107
Starting order determination, 161
Starting the race, 145, 146
Steering 67–69
Radio activation button, 67
Steering columns, 67, 68
Steering gear, 68, 69
Steering wheel, 67, 68. See also Body components
Suspension, 16, 69–73
Coil springs, 69
Control arms, 72, 74, 75
Front suspension, 68
Rear suspension, 69
Shocks, 70, 71
Steering knuckles, 72, 73
Sway bars, 71–73
Track bar, 72, 73, 76
Trailing arms, 72, 75

Team members, 81–96
Body and paint men, 87
Catch-can man, 96
Chassis specialist, 88, 89, 91
Crew chief, 88–90
Engine specialist, 90–92
Gas man, 95, 96
General mechanics, 86, 87
Jack man, 94, 95
Public relations manager, 91–93
Sponsor, 82
Spotter, 93, 94
Team manager/owner, 82, 85–89
Tire changers, 95
Tire specialists, 94, 95
Testing cars, 85, 86
Trouble, 153–158
Body damage, 158
Brake fade, 153
Engine failure, 157, 158
Ignition, 154, 157
Lost cylinder, 154
Overheating, 153, 154
Pre-detonation, 157
Weight, of car, 11, 12
Wheels and tires, 73–77, 135, 136
Winston Cup champions, 184, 185
Winston Cup race winners, 186
Winston Cup rookies of the year, 187